CONTENTS

Series/Number 07-092

UNDERSTANDING
REGRESSION ASSUMPTIONS

WILLIAM D. BERRY
Florida State University

SAGE PUBLICATIONS
International Educational and Professional Publisher
Newbury Park   London   New Delhi

For information address:

SAGE Publications, Inc.
2455 Teller Road
Newbury Park, California 91320
E-mail: order@sagepub.com

SAGE Publications Ltd.
6 Bonhill Street
London EC2A 4PU
United Kingdom

SAGE Publications India Pvt. Ltd.
M-32 Market
Greater Kailash I
New Delhi 110 048 India

Printed in the United States of America

Berry, William Dale.
    Understanding regression assumptions / William D. Berry.
      p.   cm.—(Quantitative applications in the social sciences;
92)
    Includes bibliographical references.
    ISBN 0-8039-4263-X (pbk.)
    1. Social sciences—Statistical methods.   2. Regression analysis.
3. Error analysis (Mathematics)   I. Title.   II. Series: Sage
university papers series. Quantitative applications in the social
sciences; 92.
    HA31.3.B47   1993
    300'.1'519536—dc20   92-42925

          98 99 00 01 10 9 8 7 6 5

Sage Production Editor: Diane S. Foster

When citing a university paper, please use the proper form. Remember to cite the current Sage University Paper series title and include the paper number. One of the following formats can be adapted (depending on the style manual used):
(1) BERRY, W. D. (1993) Understanding Regression Assumptions. Sage University Paper series on Quantitative Applications in the Social Sciences, 07-092. Newbury Park, CA: Sage.
OR
(2) Berry, W. D. (1993) *Understanding regression assumptions* (Sage University Paper series on Quantitative Applications in the Social Sciences, series no. 07-092). Newbury Park, CA: Sage.

SERIES EDITOR'S INTRODUCTION

Regression analysis is the fundamental tool of the trade, at least for nonexperimentalists. Still, while the most used, it is also probably the most abused. Every first-year graduate student quickly learns to estimate a basic multiple regression model, such as

$$Y = b_0 + b_1X_1 + b_2X_2 + e.$$

Suppose, for example, political scientist Betty Brown obtains the following ordinary least squares (OLS) estimates on the determinants of welfare spending in the 50 American states:

$$\hat{Y} = 543.66 + 87.10X_1 + 450.39X_2,$$

where $\hat{Y}$ = welfare expenditures (dollars per capita) in the state, X_1 = Democratic seats in the legislature (in percentage), X_2 = urban population (in percentage).

Professor Brown may conclude that for every 1% increase in Democrat seats, an increase of $87.10 is expected in welfare expenditures (with urbanization held constant). How good an estimate of the effect of X_1 is this? More precisely, is it the best linear unbiased estimate (BLUE)? If the answer is yes, then the estimate informs us of a real-world association. If the answer is no, then the estimate may describe only movement along a plane on a pencil-and-paper graph.

Obviously, then, we should seek estimates that may be described as BLUE. This we can do by meeting the regression assumptions. Professor Berry carefully defines each of these assumptions, then explains their substantive meanings. The use of good verbal description aided by well-chosen graphics and simple proofs makes accessible such problems as measurement, specification, multicollinearity, heteroscedasticity, and autocorrelation. Data for the explication come from systematic development of an equation for a variable of widespread interest—human weight.

v

Understanding the regression assumptions allows the analyst to appreciate the weaknesses, as well as the strengths, of his or her estimates. Of course, without this understanding, necessary steps toward model improvement cannot be taken. Although until now this series has had many monographs touching on the topic of regression (Lewis-Beck's *Applied Regression,* No. 22; Achen's *Interpreting and Using Regression,* No. 29; Berry & Feldman's *Multiple Regression in Practice,* No. 50; Newbold & Bos's *Stochastic Parameter Regression Models,* No. 51; Schroeder, Sjoquist, & Stephan's *Understanding Regression Analysis,* No. 57; Jaccard, Turisi, & Wan's *Interaction Effects in Multiple Regression,* No. 72; and Fox's *Regression Diagnostics,* No. 79), none has focused on the assumptions. Thus Professor Berry's contribution fills an important gap.

—*Michael S. Lewis-Beck*
Series Editor

ACKNOWLEDGMENTS

I would like to thank Isabelle Romieu and Walter Willett for their generosity in furnishing a data set that forms the basis for many illustrations in this monograph. Thanks are also due to the series editor, Michael Lewis-Beck, and to Larry Bartels, Frances Berry, Patricia Conley, Stanley Feldman, Charles Franklin, Michael Goldfield, Melissa Hardy, Gary King, Glenn Mitchell, James Stimson, Kevin Wang, and several anonymous referees for valuable comments on earlier versions. Finally, I am grateful to Roy T. St. Laurent for detecting an error in a verson of Figure 2.1 included in a previous printing of this monograph.

UNDERSTANDING REGRESSION ASSUMPTIONS

WILLIAM D. BERRY
Florida State University

1. INTRODUCTION

Numerous assumptions are made—implicitly, if not explicitly—whenever regression analysis is used in social science research.[1] Quantitative social science has become prevalent enough that nearly all second-year graduate students can recite a list of the standard regression assumptions. Yet these assumptions are often learned by rote, so that students fail to understand the "real meaning" of the assumptions. I decided to write this volume because the following type of exchange with graduate students about their research has become too familiar to me over the years:

Instructor: Do you think you might have a problem with heteroscedasticity [or any of a number of other problems—specification error, measurement error, autocorrelation, nonlinearity, or whatever] in your model?

Student: I'm not sure.

Instructor: Well, what do we mean by heteroscedasticity?

Student (confidently): The variance of the error term is not constant.

Instructor: Okay. Your dependent variable is an individual's charitable spending [or insert any other variable]. And you include the following independent variables. . . . What would it mean *in this case* if the error term were heteroscedastic?

Student (somewhat less confidently): It would mean that the variance of the error term has different values for different observations.

Instructor: But tell me what that might mean *substantively* about your model. What might it mean about charitable spending, about the independent variables in your model, about the determinants of charitable spending that you might have left out of your model, and about how all these variables are related?

Student (sensing that some gaps in his or her knowledge have been discovered): I really don't know.

1

Thus it seems that although many social scientists can confidently "rattle off" the list of assumptions of multiple regression analysis (no specification error, no measurement error, lack of autocorrelation, and so forth) and perhaps a one-sentence formal definition of each, a solid understanding of the substantive meanings of these assumptions is often lacking. And if our understanding of these assumptions is limited to knowledge of a rote definition, so that we cannot analyze whether the assumptions are met in concrete research applications, we would be just as well off not knowing the assumptions at all.

The purpose of this monograph is to describe the assumptions of regression in a way that will encourage students to get past memorizing the correct phrasing of a definition and understand how one considers whether the assumptions are actually satisfied in a particular research project. I confine the discussion to regression because of its dominance as a methodology in the social sciences, although a similar monograph could be written about any other empirical research technique. If social scientists acquire the habit of approaching regression-reliant research by giving explicit consideration to whether the regression assumptions are met in the case at hand, perhaps they will be able to apply this approach more generally when using other research techniques.

I begin with a formal review of the standard multiple regression assumptions as they are typically presented in econometrics or regression textbooks.[2] Do not be intimidated if you do not understand the meaning and significance of each of these assumptions. (If you did understand all the assumptions, you would not need to read this book!) Next, I introduce a substantive example on which I will rely throughout the monograph—a model of the determinants of human weight. I have chosen this illustration because the factors influencing a person's weight is a topic about which all of us—regardless of our specialized interests—should have reasonably good intuition. Then, I return to the regression assumptions, considering the substantive meaning of each of the assumptions individually, stressing how analysts can assess whether each assumption is met in concrete research applications.

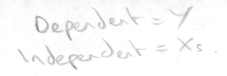

2. A FORMAL PRESENTATION
OF THE REGRESSION ASSUMPTIONS

The Regression Surface

In the standard multivariate regression model, a *dependent* variable, Y, is assumed to be a function of a set of k *independent* variables (or *regressors*), $X_1, X_2, \ldots, X_k$, in some population. The model assumes that for each set of values for the k independent variables—X_{1j}, $X_{2j}, \ldots, X_{kj}$—there is a *conditional probability distribution* of Y values such that the mean of the distribution is on the "surface" (with one independent variable, a line; with two independent variables, a plane) expressed by the equation

$$E(Y_j | X_{1j}, X_{2j}, \ldots, X_{kj}) = \alpha + \beta_1 X_{1j} + \beta_2 X_{2j} + \ldots + \beta_k X_{kj} \qquad [2.1]$$

$$= \alpha + \sum_{i=1}^{k} \beta_i X_{ij}$$

In this equation, Y_j and X_{ij} denote the values of the variables Y and X_i, respectively, for the jth observation.[3] Also, the symbol | is read "given," so that $E(Y_j | X_{1j}, X_{2j}, \ldots, X_{kj})$ denotes the mean or *expected value* of Y for cases in the population for which $X_1 = X_{1j}$, $X_2 = X_{2j}, \ldots$, and $X_k = X_{kj}$. The graph in Figure 2.1 shows the regression plane,

$$E(Y_j | X_{1j}, X_{2j}) = \alpha + \beta_1 X_{1j} + \beta_2 X_{2j},$$

for the case of two independent variables.

For the bivariate regression model with the single independent variable, X, this assumption can be represented in graph form in even greater detail. Figure 2.2 shows the conditional probability distribution of Y for three different values of X—X_1, X_2, and X_3—where probability is measured vertically. Here, the means of the distributions fall on the line

$$E(Y_j | X_j) = \alpha + \beta X_j.$$

(The fact that these conditional distributions are all sketched as being *normal* and with the same variance is a consequence of regression assumptions A8 and A6, presented below.)

Returning to the general multivariate case of Equation 2.1, the Greek letter coefficients ($\alpha, \beta_1, \beta_2, \ldots, \beta_k$) denote population coefficients or

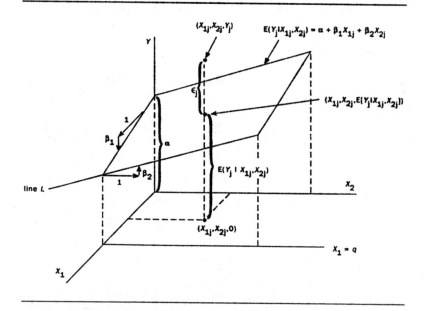

Figure 2.1. The Multiple Regression Plane With Two Independent Variables

NOTE: The position of a point in the graph of the three-dimensional space is denoted by placing the values of X_1, X_2, and Y associated with the point in parentheses and separated by commas, so that (a, b, c) denotes the point at which $X_1 = a$, $X_2 = b$, and $Y = c$.

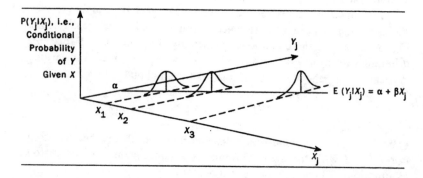

Figure 2.2. Regression Assumptions for a Bivariate Model

parameters. The *intercept,* α, is the expected value of Y when all independent variables are equal to zero. The β_i coefficients are generally called *partial slope coefficients*; for each i, the coefficient β_i can be interpreted as the change in the expected value of Y associated with a unit increase in X_i, when all other independent variables are held constant. If we include as regressors only variables that a theory suggests should be causes of the dependent variable, β_i can be interpreted as a measure of the strength of the *impact* or *effect* of X_i on Y. I shall use this interpretation freely throughout this monograph, even though readers should understand that the formal assumptions of multivariate regression do not include causality, and therefore, any justification for a "causal" interpretation of regression coefficients must be based on theory external to the regression.

In the interpretation of the meaning of β_i, it makes sense to say simply "when all other independent variables are held constant," *without specifying the values at which they are held constant,* because the functional form of Equation 2.1 makes it so that the effects of independent variables are *additive.* In an additive model, for each independent variable, X_i, when all other independent variables are held constant, the change in the expected value of Y associated with a unit increase in X_i is the same regardless of the specific values at which the other Xs are fixed. Put differently, each independent variable's effect on the dependent variable does not vary depending on the values of the other independent variables. (In a *nonadditive* model, at least two variables *interact* in influencing the dependent variable. It is said that two variables interact in determining a dependent variable, Y, if the effect of one independent variable on Y varies with the value of the other independent variable.)

The *linearity* assumption is also implicit in the functional form of Equation 2.1. X_i is said to be linearly related to Y if, when all other independent variables are held constant, the change in the expected value of Y associated with a small fixed increase in X_i is the same regardless of the value of X_i, that is, the slope of the relationship between X_i and the expected value of Y is constant. (X_i is described as *nonlinearly* related to Y if the slope of the relationship varies depending on the value of X_i.)

These interpretations of the regression coefficients are reflected for the case of two independent variables in the graph in Figure 2.1. In the graph, α is the expected value of Y when $X_1 = X_2 = 0$, β_1 can be seen to be the change in the expected value of Y resulting from a unit increase in X_1 when X_2 is held constant, and β_2 is the change in the expected value of the dependent variable when X_2 is increased by 1 and X_1 is held constant. The linearity in the model is reflected in the graph by the fact that the regression surface is a (flat) plane. Because the surface is a plane, if we hold X_1 constant at some value q, by restricting attention to those points in the vertical plane at which $X_1 = q$, and then take the intersection of this vertical plane with the regression surface, the result is a line (or *linear* curve)—depicted by line L—with constant slope β_2.

The Role of the Error Term

Although the means of the conditional probability distributions for Y are assumed by the regression model to fall exactly on the surface of Equation 2.1, the actual value of Y for an individual observation, j, is assumed determined by both the independent variables and an *error* (or *disturbance*) term ε_j, as in the equation

$$Y_j = \alpha + \beta_1 X_{1j} + \beta_2 X_{2j} + \ldots + \beta_k X_{kj} + \varepsilon_j = \alpha + \left(\sum_{i=1}^{k} \beta_i X_{ij} \right) + \varepsilon_j . \qquad [2.2]$$

Noting that Equation 2.2 can be written as

$$\varepsilon_j = Y_j - E(Y_j | X_{1j}, X_{2j}, \ldots, X_{kj}),$$

we recognize that the error term ε_j is the deviation between the observed value of Y for observation j, Y_j, and the mean value of the Y distribution for cases in the population having the X values of observation j (i.e., $X_1 = X_{1j}$, $X_2 = X_{2j}$, ..., and $X_k = X_{kj}$). The graph in Figure 2.1 illustrates the meaning of ε_j for the two-independent variable case by showing that ε_j is the vertical distance between the observed value of Y for case j and the regression plane. Nothing is more critical to an understanding of the "substantive meaning" of regression assumptions than an appreciation of the meaning of the disturbance term.

To understand the meaning of the error term, we should first consider the notion of a *true model*. In the regression literature, a true model is usually conceived as the one that explains all variation in the dependent variable in the population of interest. Alternatively, it can be viewed as the model that completely describes the process determining the value of the dependent variable for any case in the population; thus the equation reflecting the true model would include *all* variables that have an effect on the dependent variable, and accurately reflect the nature of all of these effects. It would be incredibly naive to believe that in a concrete social science application, the true model would be known, but perhaps it is more plausible to presume that this model exists, yet is unknown to the researcher.

Still, many challenge the basic premise that a given dependent variable (in a population) can be explained only one way, with a unique true model. For example, Luskin (1991) writes:

> Uniquely *true* models exist only in the assumptions of econometric proofs. A given [dependent variable] can always be explained in a number of equally valid ways—in terms of a larger set of conceptually finer [independent variables] or a smaller set of conceptually grosser ones, in terms of variables that have their effect at close quarters or variables that act from afar. At most, there may plausibly be a single true model of *a given type*—at a given level of conceptual aggregation, at a given causal distance. (p. 1038)

Luskin makes a very good point. For example, assume we seek to explain the attitude of individuals in some population about a particular issue. We can formulate explanations at a variety of "causal distances." At extremely "close quarters," we could explain the issue attitude with other more general attitudes. From a greater causal distance, we could develop a model based on an individual's social background characteristics. "From afar," we might construct a model relying on an individual's childhood experiences and socialization. Although one might argue that a true model would need to incorporate variables at each of these causal distances, such a merger may be inappropriate. For instance, if one can explain a specific attitude with a set of general attitudes, and can explain each of these general attitudes with social background characteristics, a model seeking to explain the specific attitude with both the general attitudes and social background characteristics would not be appropriate. Instead, there would be two different explanations of the specific attitude, each reflecting a different causal distance.

Another position is that even at a fixed causal distance and a fixed level of conceptual aggregation, it is fruitless to speak of true models in the context of social science research. In this view, there is no such thing as a true model; there are only theories. Consequently, it is pointless to try to assess whether a regression model conforms to some "true" model; realistically, we must confine ourselves to an analysis of whether a regression model accurately specifies *our theory* about the factors influencing some dependent variable.

I should make my position on "true models" clear. For virtually every social science dependent variable I can imagine, I doubt there is a true model. Even if there is, I am convinced that I will never be able to identify it. Thus, for the most part, it is not helpful to think about true models when conducting research. Good research is guided by focused questions that prompt the construction of theories and hypotheses. Instead of worrying about whether our regression models conform to some hypothetical "true" model—which we will never know—we ought to judge our regression models by whether they conform to our theories, and thus whether they can be used to answer our research questions. Nevertheless, to understand the meaning of an error term, it is useful, as a heuristic device, to presume that there is an unknown true model and compare the regression equation to this hypothetical model.

So assume, for the moment, that there is a true model explaining a dependent variable, Y, in a population. Undoubtedly, this would be a very "long" model, as it would contain all the variables influencing Y; presumably, some of these variables have strong impacts on Y, but there would also be many other explanatory variables, each of which has only a weak impact. One line of reasoning suggests that this true model would be fully *deterministic*; that is, it would account perfectly for the value of the dependent variable for any case in the population.[4] Given this view, the true model would take the form

$$Y_j = \mu_0 + \mu_1 E_{1j} + \mu_2 E_{2j} + \ldots + \mu_p E_{pj}, \qquad [2.3]$$

where $E_1, E_2, \ldots, E_p$ represents a finite—but very large—set of explanatory variables.[5]

But most regression textbooks maintain that even true models are not fully deterministic, because there is "bound to be some 'intrinsic' randomness" in human behavior that cannot be explained with other variables (Gujarati, 1988, p. 34; see also Greene, 1990, p. 144; Johnson, Johnson, & Buse, 1987, pp. 43-44). This inherent randomness is sometimes attributed to a "free will component" of human behavior, or to the influence of completely "unpredictable events" (Kelejian & Oates, 1989, p. 45). A counterargument is that what we label as "inherent randomness" in behavior is more accurately described as that part of the behavior of the dependent variable that, at the moment, we are not yet prepared to explain. In this view, the introduction of a random component into a true model means that the model is not really "true." In any event, we modify our initial formulation of the true model by adding a variable R, which represents any inherently random component in the behavior of Y, to obtain

$$Y_j = \mu_0 + \mu_1 E_{1j} + \mu_2 E_{2j} + \ldots + \mu_p E_{pj} + R_j, \quad \text{[the true model]} \quad [2.4]$$

where together the Es and R fully account for variation in Y in the population. (If one prefers the earlier deterministic version of the true model, one need only assume that $R = 0$, thereby rendering Equation 2.4 identical to Equation 2.3.)

In the practical research setting, it is reasonable to assume that we would never be able to undertake empirical analysis of the true model. We would always have to exclude some (indeed, most) of the Es in Equation 2.4 and arrive at an estimation regression model including one or more independent variables and an error term:

$$Y_j = \alpha + \beta_1 X_{1j} + \beta_2 X_{2j} + \ldots + \beta_k X_{kj} + \varepsilon_j. \quad \text{[the estimation model]} \quad [2.5]$$

For clarity, we shall relabel those explanatory variables from the true model that are deleted from the estimation model of Equation 2.5 as Zs—so as to distinguish clearly between *included* (the Xs) and *excluded* (the Zs) variables. Then, we can rewrite Equation 2.4 dividing the Es into separate groupings of k Xs and m Zs (where $k + m = p$, but k is much smaller than m), and renaming the partial slope coefficients for Zs with δs:

$$Y_j = \mu_0 + (\beta_1 X_{1j} + \beta_2 X_{2j} + \ldots + \beta_k X_{kj}) + (\delta_1 Z_{1j} + \delta_2 Z_{2j} + \ldots + \delta_m Z_{mj}) + R_j$$

$$= \mu_0 + \left(\sum_{i=1}^{k} \beta_i X_{ij} \right) + \left(\sum_{i=1}^{m} \delta_i Z_{ij} \right) + R_j.$$

Then, we manipulate this equation to isolate the Xs on one side:

$$\sum_{i=1}^{k} \beta_i X_{ij} = (Y_j - \mu_0) - \left(\sum_{i=1}^{m} \delta_i Z_{ij} \right) - R_j. \quad [2.6]$$

Next, we rewrite estimation model 2.5, isolating the error term on the left-hand side:

$$\varepsilon_j = Y_j - \alpha - (\beta_1 X_{1j} + \beta_2 X_{2j} + \ldots + \beta_k X_{kj}) = Y_j - \alpha - \left(\sum_{i=1}^{k} \beta_i X_{ij} \right). \quad [2.7]$$

Finally, substituting the expression for $\sum_{i=1}^{k} \beta_i X_{ij}$ from Equation 2.6 into Equation 2.7 yields

$$\varepsilon_j = Y_j - \alpha - Y_j + \mu_0 + \left(\sum_{i=1}^{m} \delta_i Z_{ij} \right) + R_j = (\mu_0 - \alpha) + \left(\sum_{i=1}^{m} \delta_i Z_{ij} \right) + R_j. \quad [2.8]$$

Equation 2.8 implies that we can interpret the error term in a regression model as the combined impact of all variables that affect the dependent variable but are not included among the regressors, plus a "random variable" representing any intrinsically random component in the behavior of the dependent variable. Therefore, assuming we can never include all the variables that would be in a true model in any estimation equation, all regression models must include an error term that accounts for the effects of excluded variables.

Although it is probably obvious why, in any concrete application of regression, one will always have to exclude some variables that actually influence the dependent variable, it is useful to identify explicitly the reasons such exclusions are made. First, many factors influencing the dependent variable have such weak impacts that it is wise to ignore them. On the surface, it might seem that there is a strong rationale for including *all* variables thought to have impacts on the dependent variable, even if the impacts are expected to be weak. This is because (a) certain variables hypothesized to have weak effects may actually have stronger effects that would be missed if the variables were excluded, and (b) even if the effect of a variable were weak, the inclusion of the variable allows for a test of the proposition that the impact is weak. But there are substantial costs to including in a regression a variable having only a weak effect on the dependent variable. We will see in Chapter 5 that if the variable having a weak impact is highly correlated with other regressors in the equation that have a much stronger impact, the inclusion of the "weak" variable will increase the variability of our estimates of the partial slope coefficients for the "strong" variables. Indeed, in many situations, if *all* factors influencing the dependent variable were included in a regression, the number of independent variables would exceed the number of cases available for estimation; we will see later that this leads to *perfect multicollinearity,* which violates the assumptions of regression and makes it impossible to obtain meaningful estimates of the partial slope coefficients of the model.

Second, even if all variables thought to have weak effects on the dependent variable are excluded from a regression model, there still may be a sufficient number of variables with strong effects on the dependent variable, and sufficiently high correlations among these variables, to make coefficient estimates highly imprecise. If so, theory becomes essential in deciding which of the set of variables with strong impacts to include and which to exclude. Presumably, not all of the explanatory variables with strong impacts on the dependent variable are of equal theoretical interest. For example, assume the principal objective is to obtain accurate estimates of the effects of four variables—say, X_1, X_2, X_3, and X_4—on Y. If so (as Chapter 5 will show), it is better to exclude independent variables that are weakly correlated with the four variables than variables having high correlations with these Xs.

A third reason for excluding a variable from a regression is lack of data. There may be some *specific* variables that are inherently unobservable in some sample. Also, although we tend to be reluctant to admit that our research choices are sometimes dictated by resource availability, there may be financial or time constraints that make it impractical to measure a variable that, given vast resources, could be measured. These same constraints may also limit the overall *number* of independent variables for which data can be gathered, thereby forcing the exclusion of some variables.

Finally, there is ignorance. Even if a variable has a powerful influence on the dependent variable, if the theory motivating the regression model does not point to this explanatory variable, the variable naturally would be excluded.

In any event, when considering whether the assumptions of regression concerning the error term are met in a substantive application, we shall frequently return to this conception of the error term as representing the combined impacts of all variables influencing the dependent variable but that are not included in the regression, plus any intrinsic random component in the behavior of the dependent variable.

Other Regression Assumptions

In addition to the assumptions inherent in the form of Equation 2.2, several other assumptions about the natures of the disturbance term, the dependent variable, and the independent variables are made in the standard regression model:

A1. All *independent* variables $(X_1, X_2, \ldots, X_k)$ are *quantitative* or *dichotomous*, and the *dependent* variable, Y, is *quantitative, continuous*, and *unbounded*.[6] Moreover, all variables are measured without error.

A2. All independent variables have *nonzero variance* (i.e., each independent variable has some variation in value).

A3. There is not *perfect multicollinearity* (i.e., there is no exact linear relationship between two or more of the independent variables).

A4. At each set of values for the k independent variables, $(X_{1j}, X_{2j}, \ldots, X_{kj})$, $E(\varepsilon_j | X_{1j}, X_{2j}, \ldots, X_{kj}) = 0$ (i.e., the mean value of the error term is zero).

A5. For each X_i, $COV(X_{ij}, \varepsilon_j) = 0$ (i.e., each independent variable is uncorrelated with the error term).[7]

A6. At each set of values for the k independent variables, $(X_{1j}, X_{2j}, \ldots, X_{kj})$, $VAR(\varepsilon_j | X_{1j}, X_{2j}, \ldots, X_{kj}) = \sigma^2$, where σ^2 is a constant (i.e., the conditional variance of the error term is constant); this is known as the assumption of *homoscedasticity*.

A7. For any two observations, $(X_{1j}, X_{2j}, \ldots, X_{kj})$ and $(X_{1h}, X_{2h}, \ldots, X_{kh})$, $COV(\varepsilon_j, \varepsilon_h) = 0$ (i.e., error terms for different observations are uncorrelated); this assumption is known as a lack of *autocorrelation*.[8]

A8. At each set of values for the k independent variables, ε_j is normally distributed.

As a set, A1 through A7 are referred to as the *Gauss-Markov assumptions*.

Equation 2.2 is the population regression equation, the parameters of which are unknown. However, given a sample of data from the population, these parameters can be estimated. Most commonly, *least squares* estimators—or OLS (ordinary least squares) estimators—are determined.[9] To make certain that population parameters are clearly distinguished from their estimators, I will denote the OLS estimator of the intercept α by a, and the estimator of the partial slope coefficient β_i by b_i.

If the Gauss-Markov assumptions (A1 through A7) are met, least squares estimators have several desirable properties (e.g., unbiasedness and efficiency), and also can be used appropriately for statistical inference (e.g., to conduct tests of statistical significance or construct confidence intervals). These desirable properties are delineated in Chapter 4.

3. A "WEIGHTY" ILLUSTRATION

To illustratè the "substantive meanings" of the regression assumptions, throughout this monograph I will explore a regression model explaining human weight in a population of 134 women, aged 34 to 59. And I will assume that we are privileged—as we are not in the real world of research—to know the population parameters of the *true* model:[10]

$$\text{WEIGHT}_j = \alpha + \beta_C \text{CALORIES}_j + \beta_F \text{FAT}_j + \beta_E \text{EXERCISE}_j \quad [3.1]$$
$$+ \beta_H \text{HEIGHT}_j + \beta_A \text{AGE}_j + \beta_S \text{SMOKER}_j$$
$$+ \beta_{FF} \text{FAT}_j^2 + \beta_{SE}[(\text{SMOKER}_j)(\text{EXERCISE}_j)]$$
$$+ \beta_M \text{METABOLISM}_j + \varepsilon_{wj},$$

where all Gauss-Markov assumptions are satisfied[11] and the variables are defined as follows: WEIGHT is human weight measured in pounds, CALORIES is average daily food intake (for the previous year) measured in calories, FAT is average daily saturated fat intake (for the previous year) measured in grams, EXERCISE is average daily energy expenditure from vigorous physical activity (for the previous year) measured in calories, HEIGHT is height in inches, AGE is age in years, SMOKER is a dichotomous variable that equals 1 for a smoker and 0 for a nonsmoker, METABOLISM is metabolic rate measured in "luckies,"[12] and ε_w is the error term. The population parameters are as follows: α (the intercept) = 38.10; β_C (for CALORIES) = 0.0291; β_F (for FAT) = -3.098; β_E (for EXERCISE) = -0.1183; β_H (for HEIGHT) = 1.346; β_A (for AGE) = -0.285; β_S (for SMOKER) = 3.01; β_{FF} (for FAT^2) = 0.084; β_{SE} (for SMOKER • EXERCISE) = 0.1097; and β_M (for METABOLISM) = -1.795.

In this hypothetical population, there are two determinants of weight that are positive and *linear* in their impact: height and food intake. The coefficient of 1.346 for HEIGHT indicates that 1 inch increase in height is associated with an increase in expected weight of nearly 1.35 pounds when all other independent variables are held constant. The value for β_C of .0291 implies that, with all other variables held constant, an increase in average daily food intake of 100 calories results, on average, in a weight increase of 2.91 (= 100 • .0291) pounds. Note that when speaking of *increases* in height, food intake, and weight in these interpretations, we refer to *cross-sectional* "increases," that is, increases in the value of a variable from one unit in the population to another or, in this case, from one woman to another. We are more used to thinking about "change" in the *dynamic* sense, in which we refer to increases or decreases in the value of a variable within a single unit over time. When conducting *time-series* regression—that is, when the sample for estimation consists of observations of a single unit at multiple points in time—it is appropriate to give partial slope coefficients a dynamic interpretation. It can also be tempting to give dynamic interpretations to the partial slope coefficients of a cross-sectional regression, that is, one that reflects relationships across units observed at a single point in time. For example, someone interested in assessing the effectiveness of dieting might hazard an inference—based on the coefficient, β_C, that describes the relationship between food intake and weight across women—that any woman in the population can be expected to lose 2.91 pounds if she reduces her average daily food consumption by 100 calories, while holding all other independent variables constant. But we are justified in drawing over-time inferences from cross-sectional regression coefficients only when assumptions beyond those introduced in Chapter 2 are met. These further assumptions are discussed in Chapter 5.

Two determinants in the regression model are linearly but negatively related to weight: age and metabolic rate. An increase of one decade in age is associated with a decrease in expected weight of 2.85 (= 10 • .285) pounds, when all other variables are fixed. A faster metabolic rate leads to lower weight; in particular, an increase of one lucky in metabolic rate is associated with an average weight reduction of about 1.80 pounds (when other variables are held constant).

Finally, one independent variable, fat intake, is *nonlinearly* related to weight, and two other variables—whether or not a woman smokes and the amount of vigorous exercise she gets—interact in influencing weight. This might seem to be at odds with the claim in Chapter 2 that the assumptions of *linearity* and *additivity* are inherent in the functional form of Equation 2.2. However, some nonlinear and/or nonadditive models are said to be *intrinsically linear and additive*; for such models, a mathematical transformation yields an equation that is both linear and additive, so that the nonlinearity and/or nonadditivity specified is consistent with the standard OLS regression model. I will discuss nonlinearity and nonadditivity in greater depth in Chapter 5; for now, I simply note that the weight model of Equation 3.1 is intrinsically linear and additive, and turn to an interpretation of the specific natures of the nonlinearity and nonadditivity reflected in the model.

Like overall food intake, the consumption of saturated fat is positively related to weight, but this relationship is nonlinear. It is the inclusion of the term FAT^2 (i.e., the square of the variable FAT) that results in a nonlinear specification. Figure 3.1 presents a graph of the relationship specified in Equation 3.1 between average daily fat intake and the expected value of weight (when all other variables in the equation are fixed at their mean value in the population). The range of saturated fat intake in this artificially rigged "population" is roughly from 20 to 50 grams. And the graph shows that throughout this substantively meaningful range of FAT values, the strength of the *effect* of saturated fat consumption on weight increases as the level of consumption increases. Indeed, from Equation 3.1 we can determine that, when all other independent variables are held constant,[13]

at any fixed value of fat intake, FAT*, the slope of the relationship between FAT and the expected value of WEIGHT

[3.2]

$$= \beta_F + (2\beta_{FF} \cdot FAT^*) = -3.098 + [(2)(.084)(FAT^*)] = -3.098 + (.168)(FAT^*).$$

So, for example, when saturated fat intake is 20 grams/day, the formula yields a slope of .26 [= -3.098 + (.168)(20)], indicating that an increase of 1 gram/day in saturated fat intake results in an average weight increase of .26 pounds, when all other independent variables are held constant. In comparison, at a fat intake level of 30 grams/day, the same increase of 1 gram/day leads to an expected increase of 1.94 pounds.

The two variables in Equation 3.1 that interact in determining a woman's weight are whether or not she smokes and the amount of vigorous exercise she gets. To review the definition, when two independent variables interact in influencing a dependent variable Y, the strength of the effect of one independent variable on Y depends on the value of the other independent variable.[14] It is the product term, SMOKER • EXERCISE, in Equation 3.1 that makes the model interactive. Given the interaction, the typical interpretation of the partial slope coefficient—as the change in the expected value of the dependent variable associated with a unit increase in an independent variable, holding the rest of the independent variables constant—does not apply to the coefficients, β_E and β_S (for SMOKER and EXERCISE). To determine the correct interpretation of the coefficients relating to the effects of smoking and exercise, we "evaluate" Equation 3.1 separately for smokers and nonsmokers. We do this for *nonsmokers* by "fixing" SMOKER at zero; that is, we set $SMOKER_j = 0$ in the

16

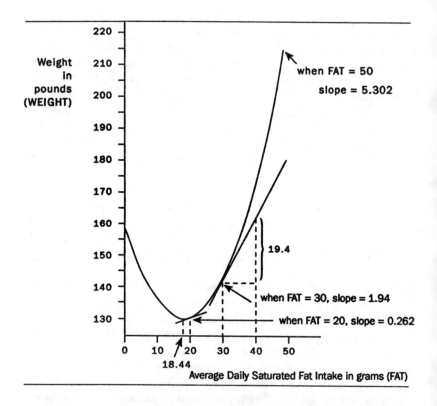

Figure 3.1. The Nonlinear Relationship Between Saturated Fat Intake and the Expected Value of Weight (Specified in Equation 3.1)
NOTE: This figure represents the situation when all other variables are fixed at their mean value in the population (i.e., CALORIES = 1,645, EXERCISE = 20.9, HEIGHT = 64.5, AGE = 46.8, SMOKER = .30, METABOLISM = 0, and SMOKER • EXERCISE = 5.3).

equation. This means that SMOKER • EXERCISE also becomes zero, so that both these regressors "drop out," and the equation simplifies to

$$\text{WEIGHT}_j = \alpha + \beta_C\text{CALORIES}_j + \beta_F\text{FAT}_j + \beta_E\text{EXERCISE}_j \qquad [3.3]$$
$$+ \beta_H\text{HEIGHT}_j + \beta_A\text{AGE}_j + \beta_{FF}\text{FAT}_j^2$$
$$+ \beta_M\text{METABOLISM}_j + \varepsilon_{Wj}.$$

Then we evaluate Equation 3.1 for *smokers* by setting SMOKER = 1; simplifying and combining terms, we get

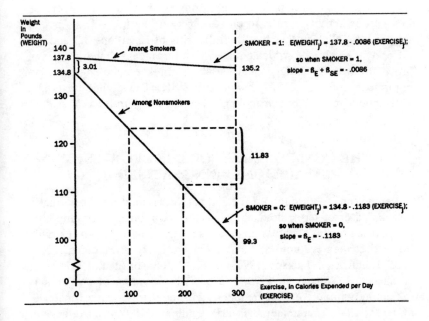

Figure 3.2. The Interaction Between Whether a Woman Smokes and Amount of Exercise in Influencing the Expected Value of Weight (Specified in Equation 3.1)
NOTE: The particular lines graphed here reflect the situation in which all other variables are fixed at their mean value in the population (i.e., CALORIES = 1,645, HEIGHT = 64.5, AGE = 46.8, META-BOLISM = 0, and FAT = 25.2). However, the slopes of the two lines do not vary depending on the values at which the other variables are fixed; only the intercepts of the two lines so vary.

$$WEIGHT_j = (\alpha + \beta_S) + \beta_C CALORIES_j + \beta_F FAT_j \qquad [3.4]$$
$$+ (\beta_E + \beta_{SE})EXERCISE_j + \beta_H HEIGHT_j + \beta_A AGE_j$$
$$+ \beta_{FF} FAT_j^2 + \beta_M METABOLISM_j + \varepsilon_{Wj}.$$

Equations 3.3 and 3.4 show that the weight model of Equation 3.1 is one in which the slope of the relationship between amount of exercise and expected weight is different among smokers and nonsmokers (when the remaining independent variables are held constant); this is depicted in the graph shown in Figure 3.2. Among nonsmokers, this slope is β_E (which equals −.1183); among smokers it is $\beta_E + \beta_{SE}$ (which is −.1183 + .1097 = −.0086). Thus, among *nonsmokers,* an increase in energy expenditure from vigorous exercise of 100 calories/day leads to an expected weight reduction of 11.83 (= 100 • β_E) pounds, when all other independent variables are fixed. But among *smokers,* the same increase in vigorous activity results in only a .86 (= 100 • [$\beta_E + \beta_{SE}$]) pound weight loss. Note further that the intercepts of Equations 3.3 and 3.4 differ by the value β_S (which equals 3.01); this means that at any fixed levels for the other independent variables, smokers who engage in no vigorous exercise (i.e., for which EXERCISE = 0) weigh, on average, 3.01 pounds more than *non*smokers who get no vigorous exercise.

4. THE CONSEQUENCES OF THE REGRESSION ASSUMPTIONS BEING SATISFIED

If assumptions A1 through A7 (i.e., all but the assumption of a normally distributed error term) hold, the *Gauss-Markov theorem* ensures that OLS estimators for a regression model's coefficients have two desirable properties: they are unbiased and efficient (Berry & Feldman, 1985, p. 15; Hanushek & Jackson, 1977, pp. 46-47; Johnson et al., 1987, p. 51; Wonnacott & Wonnacott, 1979, p. 27).[15] The meaning of *unbiased* is exceedingly important, but frequently misunderstood. An estimator $\hat{\theta}$, of the population parameter, θ, is termed unbiased if its mean value over an infinite number of repeated random samples is equal to the parameter being estimated, that is, if $E(\hat{\theta}) = \theta$. Moreover, an unbiased estimator $\hat{\theta}$ of θ is called *efficient* if it has the smallest variance among a specified set of unbiased estimators. So, of the four probability distributions (for estimators $\hat{\theta}_1$, $\hat{\theta}_2$, $\hat{\theta}_3$, and $\hat{\theta}_4$) shown in Figure 4.1, both $\hat{\theta}_2$ and $\hat{\theta}_4$ are "centered" at the population parameter θ, and are therefore unbiased. The estimator $\hat{\theta}_1$ is *negatively* biased, as $E(\hat{\theta}_1) - \theta < 0$, and the estimator $\hat{\theta}_3$ is *positively* biased. And among the two unbiased estimators, $\hat{\theta}_2$ and $\hat{\theta}_4$, $\hat{\theta}_4$ is efficient, as it has the lowest variance or, alternatively, the highest *precision.*[16]

The Gauss-Markov assumptions' (A1 through A7) assurance that least squares estimators of regression coefficients are unbiased implies, in essence, that the OLS estimators are, *on average,* "on target." But this property of OLS estimators in no way ensures that an *individual* estimate of a regression parameter based on a *single* sample will equal its population value. Instead, repeated sampling from a population will produce a probability distribution of estimates for each parameter— called a *sampling distribution*—the mean of which will be the population parameter, but that will also include values higher and lower than the population parameter.[17] Moreover, the least squares estimator of a

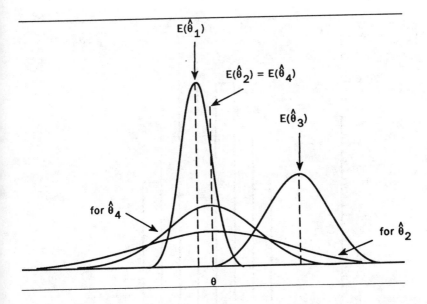

Figure 4.1. Probability Distributions of Four Different Estimators of a Parameter θ

regression parameter is guaranteed to have the smallest-variance sampling distribution among the set of estimators that are linear and unbiased, and consequently is efficient. In shorthand notation, OLS coefficient estimators are described as BLUE—the *best* (in the sense of smallest sampling variance) *l*inear *u*nbiased *e*stimators.

The importance of the assumption that the error term is normally distributed (A8) lies primarily in the information it provides about the "shapes" of the sampling distributions for regression coefficient estimators. When, in addition to assumptions A1 through A7, the assumption of a normally distributed disturbance term holds, the sampling distribution for each OLS regression coefficient estimator will also be normally distributed. Consequently, if assumptions A1 through A8 are met, the sampling distribution for the OLS estimator b_i (of β_i) is accurately reflected in the normal probability distribution for $\hat{\theta}_2$ in Figure 4.1 (where $\hat{\theta}_2 = b_i$ and $\theta = \beta_i$).

To illustrate the fact that being unbiased is a property of the *expected value* of a least squares estimator over a large (indeed, infinite) number of random samples, and *not* a property of an *individual* estimate, I took

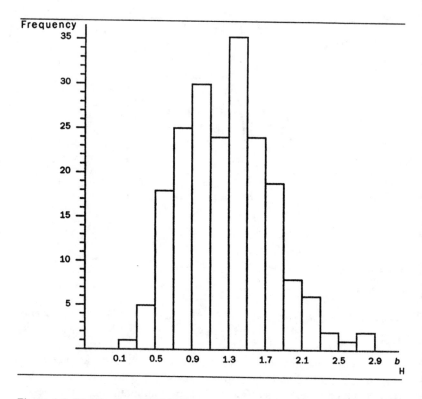

Figure 4.2. Distribution of 200 Estimates of Coefficient for HEIGHT in Weight Model

200 random samples of size 50 from the contrived population of 134 women and, with each, used OLS to estimate the parameters of Equation 3.1. Table 4.1 compares, for each regression coefficient, the average OLS estimate over the 200 samples (in Column 2) to the true population value (in Column 1). For each parameter, the average OLS estimate is quite close to the population value. Indeed, as Column 3 shows, the ratio of average estimate to parameter is uniformly near 1.00, ranging from .945 to 1.112 across parameters. But note that estimates based on a single sample have the potential to mislead greatly; for each parameter, the minimum and maximum least squares estimates across the 200 samples are reported in Columns 4 and 5, respectively. Furthermore, Figure 4.2 presents the frequency distribution for the 200 estimates of

TABLE 4.1

Comparison of OLS Estimates of Equation 3.1
to Population Parameters

Parameter	(1) Population Value[a]	(2) Average OLS Estimate[b]	(3) Column 2/ Column 1	(4) Minimum OLS Estimate[b]	(5) Maximum OLS Estimate[b]
α	38.10	40.69	1.068	−30.20	118.68
β_C	0.0291	0.0295	1.013	0.0163	0.0449
β_F	−3.098	−3.176	1.025	−5.883	−1.220
β_E	−0.1183	−0.1315	1.112	−0.2225	−0.0208
β_H	1.346	1.327	0.986	0.130	2.706
β_A	−0.285	−0.300	1.053	−0.575	0.092
β_S	3.01	2.91	0.967	−4.78	10.03
β_{FF}	0.084	0.085	1.012	0.043	0.130
β_{SE}	0.1097	0.1037	0.945	−0.1298	0.3208
β_M	−1.795	−1.814	1.011	2.456	−1.244

NOTES: a. As presented in the text.
b. Over 200 random samples of size 50.

the coefficient β_H for HEIGHT. It illustrates that whereas quite inaccurate estimates of β_H are possible based on a single random sample (estimates as low as 0.130 and as high as 2.706), estimates closer to the mean of the distribution (1.327) are much more likely. If the number of estimates reflected in such a frequency distribution would approach infinity, the distribution would become a closer and closer approximation of a normal distribution.

Keep in mind that the "best" linear unbiased estimators produced by OLS regression when the Gauss-Markov assumptions are met are not guaranteed to be best *overall*—just "best" among the class of linear *unbiased* estimators. And it is not the case that every *unbiased* estimator is better than every *biased* estimator. Indeed, when judging the overall quality of an estimator, analysts should take into account both bias and variance. For example, $\hat{\theta}_2$ in Figure 4.1 is an *un*biased estimator of θ, whereas $\hat{\theta}_1$ is biased. But $\hat{\theta}_1$ is the better estimator, in the sense that for a *single sample*, the value of $\hat{\theta}_1$ is likelier than the value of $\hat{\theta}_2$ to be close to the population value, θ. In the chapters that follow, we will see that some violations of the regression assumptions lead to bias in OLS estimators, whereas estimators remain unbiased in the face of other violations. But in most cases in which estimators remain unbiased, there is still a price to be paid in terms of precision. Therefore, one must not assume that just because OLS estimators remain unbiased when a particular regression assumption is violated, the effects of the violation are unimportant. As is obvious from the distribution of unbiased estimator $\hat{\theta}_2$, in Figure 4.1, one should derive little consolation from the fact that an estimator with a large variance happens to be unbiased.

5. THE SUBSTANTIVE MEANING
OF REGRESSION ASSUMPTIONS

Drawing Dynamic Inferences
From Cross-Sectional Regressions

As noted in Chapter 2, regression models can be *cross-sectional* (where the cases for analysis are multiple units observed at a single point in time) or *time-series* (where the cases are observations of a single unit at multiple points in time).[18] The partial slope coefficients from a cross-sectional regression model provide information about the expected change (or difference) in a dependent variable when independent variables "change" (i.e., differ) by given amounts *from one unit to another* at a single point in time. In contrast, the coefficients from a time-series regression model tell us about *dynamic* or *over-time* change; that is, they indicate the responsiveness of a dependent variable to a change in the value of an independent variable *from one time point to another* within a single unit. As the data necessary for time-series regressions are often unavailable, most social science regression analysis is cross-sectional, where the cases for analysis are individuals, households, firms, other organizations, cities, states, or nations. But in most cases, regression coefficients having dynamic interpretations tend to be more interesting.

As an example, consider research to test the hypothesis that an increase in income produces an increase in job satisfaction. The assertion that income *influences* job satisfaction usually is meant to imply that if we could select a person and intervene to increase his or her income, while holding all other variables constant, his or her job satisfaction would also rise. Typically, we would study this proposition cross-sectionally because of the difficulty of collecting time-series data about an individual's job satisfaction over a long period of time. However, even though practical constraints may force a shift to cross-sectional analysis, it is still the dynamic relationship between an individual's income and his or her job satisfaction in which we are fundamentally interested. In public policy analysis, the primary interest is also in research findings that allow dynamic interpretations. For instance, a conclusion that Policy A enhances the quality of life of citizens in a community more so than Policy B is of very limited value to policy-makers or scholars if it merely implies a cross-sectional relationship in which government jurisdictions with Policy A have a higher average quality of life than do jurisdictions with Policy B. The conclusion would be of much greater theoretical and practical significance if it implied that a jurisdiction's quality of life would be increased if *its* government's policy were changed from B to A.

This is not to say that cross-sectional relationships are completely uninteresting to social scientists. If they were, our theories of individual behavior would never include intrinsically stable characteristics—such as gender or race—as independent variables, because variables that never change in value have no time-series relationship with *any* other variable. Indeed, imposing a dynamic interpretation on the partial slope coefficient for the variable race in a regression model with political party identification as dependent variable would yield a nonsensical conclusion that begins, "As a person's race changes from white to African American, the strength of his or her identification with the Democratic party . . . "

In any event, under what conditions is it appropriate to draw dynamic inferences from the partial slope coefficients of a cross-sectional regression model? Two assumptions must be satisfied. The first is *cross-unit invariance:* The "process" determining variation in the value of the dependent variable within a unit over time must be the same from one cross-sectional unit analyzed to the next. More formally, the regression equation that expresses the cross-sectional relationships among variables must accurately specify the process determining the value of the dependent variable within every unit. The second assumption required is *cross-time invariance:* The process determining variation in the value of the dependent variable within any unit must be stable over time. In particular, the magnitude of the effect of each independent variable (and, therefore, each partial slope coefficient) must remain the same. If both these assumptions are met, observing two units that have different values for some independent variable X_1—say, X_1' and X_1''—at the same point in time gives us information identical to what we would have obtained had we been able to observe a single unit when its X_1 value was X_1' and then again later when its value had changed to X_1''. Because it is inconceivable that the assumptions of cross-unit and cross-time invariance would be satisfied *strictly* in any substantive application, the real issue is whether the assumptions are met approximately. Researchers should resist drawing dynamic inferences from cross-sectional regression coefficients unless they believe that the process determining the dependent variable is highly similar across both time and space.

The Assumption of the Absence of Perfect Multicollinearity

When there is *perfect* multicollinearity among the observations for independent variables in a sample, an infinite number of regression surfaces (e.g., regression planes in the case of two independent variables) "fit" the observed values for the dependent variable equally well, and therefore the least squares criterion fails to yield unique coefficient estimators. This is rarely a problem in the research setting, because perfect multicollinearity requires that in the sample one independent variable, say, X_i, be an *exact* linear combination of the other independent variables. This would mean that X_i could be expressed as

$$X_{ij} = c_0 + c_1 X_{1j} + c_2 X_{2j} + \ldots + c_{i-1} X_{i-1,j} + c_{i+1} X_{i+1,j} + \ldots + c_k X_{kj},$$

where some, but not all, of the constants $c_0, c_1, c_2, \ldots, c_{i-1}, c_{i+1}, \ldots, c_k$ may be zero. In this situation, if X_i were regressed on the remaining independent variables, the R^2 would be 1.00 exactly.

To illustrate the consequences of perfect multicollinearity, I examine a two-independent variable model

$$Y_j = \alpha + \beta_1 X_{1j} + \beta_2 X_{2j} + \varepsilon_j,$$

where X_1 is linearly related to X_2 according to the equation

$$X_{1j} = c + d X_{2j}. \qquad [5.1]$$

Recall that β_2 is interpreted as the change in the expected value of Y associated with a unit increase in X_2 when X_1 is held constant. But if X_1 and X_2 are related according to Equation 5.1, it would be impossible to increase X_2 by one unit *while holding X_1 constant*. Specifically, if X_2

were increased by 1, then X_1 would be increased by d units. For this reason, it is not possible to isolate the effect of one of the independent variables on the dependent variable, controlling for the other.

In practice, perfect multicollinearity will occur in only three kinds of cases. One is when an analyst mistakenly includes a set of independent variables that have a "built-in" linear relationship among them. For example, if one were to add year of birth (to be denoted YEAR) to the independent variables in Equation 3.1, there would be perfect multi-collinearity in any sample, as for all individuals,

$$AGE_j = c - d\,YEAR_j,$$

where c is the current year, and $d = 1$. A similar situation would occur if an analyst were to add a "life-style" index to the independent variables in the weight model, and the new variable were an additive index formed from calories consumed (CALORIES), amount of vigorous exercise (EXERCISE), and whether the individual smokes (SMOKER), as the index would be an exact linear combination of three other independent variables in the model.

A second situation that can lead to perfect multicollinearity is a mistake in handling dummy variables when incorporating discrete independent variables into a regression model. Perfect multicollinearity results when one succumbs to the temptation to include r dummy variables to reflect the effect of a discrete variable with r values. Instead, only $r - 1$ dummies should be used. We can see the impact of too many dummies by considering a regression involving a three-category variable reflecting the marital status of adults: (a) currently married, (b) divorced or widowed, and (c) never married. The effect of marital status can be suitably incorporated into a regression model by including *any two* of the following dichotomous variables:

$M_j = 1$ if individual j is currently married, and 0 otherwise;

$D_j = 1$ if individual j is divorced or widowed, and 0 otherwise; and

$N_j = 1$ if individual j has never been married, and 0 otherwise.

But if an analyst were to include all three of these dummy variables in a regression, perfect multicollinearity would result, because each of the three dummies is an exact linear combination of the other two. In particular,

$$M_j = 1 - (1)D_j - (1)N_j. \qquad [5.2]$$

To verify that Equation 5.2 holds, we first recognize that the marital status variable distinguishes three types of persons who have the following values on the three dummy variables:

Type of Person	M	D	N
currently married	1	0	0
never married	0	0	1
divorced or widowed	0	1	0

Then, we can confirm that the relationship among M, D, and N in Equation 5.2 is satisfied for all three types of persons. For married people, Equation 5.2 yields $1 = 1 - 0 - 0$; for those who have never married, the equation gives $0 = 1 - 0 - 1$; and for divorced or widowed persons, we get $0 = 1 - 1 - 0$.

In both of the situations discussed that lead to perfect multicollinearity, note that the problem is with the model's specification, and not with the nature of the data used for estimation. Indeed, in these situations, no data set—no matter how large—would allow OLS regression to generate unique parameter estimators. Econometricians refer to models that by virtue of their specification cannot yield unique coefficient estimators as *unidentified*.

A third situation that will lead to perfect multicollinearity occurs not because a model fails to be identified, but because the sample size for estimation is too small. Specifically, whenever the number of observations is smaller than the number of variables (dependent and independent) in the equation, there will be perfect multicollinearity. For instance, an attempt to estimate the weight model of Equation 3.1, which contains 10 variables, with data for fewer than 10 cases would fail to produce unique parameter estimators.

A geometric interpretation of a regression model with two independent variables helps clarify why having too few observations leads to multicollinearity. Assume a researcher desired to estimate a revised weight model with just HEIGHT and CALORIES as predictors. The population regression equation in this case is a plane (i.e., flat surface) in the three-dimensional space with axes showing the values of cases on CALORIES, HEIGHT, and WEIGHT. If the researcher tried to estimate this equation using only two cases, the data would be represented by two points in space. Thus the estimation task would be to find the plane in three-dimensional space that best fits these two points. The line passing through the two points fits the points perfectly. So any of the infinite number of planes that contain the line will also fit the points perfectly, and thus an infinite set of coefficient estimators will give a regression equation with an R^2 of 1.00.

One common misconception is that any "exact" relationship among independent variables (linear or nonlinear) results in perfect multicollinearity. This is not the case. Indeed, including two variables, one of which is even an exact monotonic (i.e., order-preserving), but nonlinear, transformation of the other does not result in perfect multicollinearity. For example, the inclusion of both FAT and FAT^2 in Equation 3.1 does not.

Another prevalent misconception is that high (but not perfect) multicollinearity violates the assumptions of multiple regression. But, as a review of the Gauss-Markov assumptions shows, a *nearly* linear relationship among independent variables does not violate any assumption. Therefore, even in the face of severe multicollinearity, OLS parameter estimators remain BLUE. This does not mean that analysts pay no price for the presence of high multicollinearity. Under such conditions, the standard errors for partial slope coefficient estimators for variables among the collinear set will be quite high, so that the estimates of the effects of independent variables will fluctuate considerably from sample to sample.[19] In essence, whereas perfect multicollinearity is frequently an *identification* problem, less-than-perfect multicollinearity is a *statistical* problem in which correlations among the independent variables in the *estimation sample* are too large to allow for precise estimates of the unique effects of independent variables.

The Assumption That the Error Term Is Uncorrelated With Each of the Independent Variables

It is not unusual for analysts to confuse the meanings of an *error term* in a regression equation and the OLS regression *residuals.* Residuals are defined as the differences between *observed* values of the dependent variable and *predicted* values based on the least squares coefficient estimates from a sample. More formally, if the coefficients of Equation 2.2 were estimated for a sample of cases, and these estimates were denoted $a, b_1, b_2, \ldots, b_k$, the regression residual for any case, j—to be denoted e_j—is defined by

$$e_j = Y_j - \hat{Y}_j = Y_j - (a + b_1 X_{1j} + b_2 X_{2j} + \ldots + b_k X_{kj}),$$

28

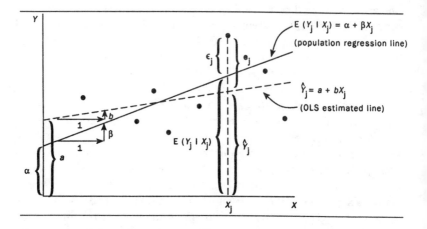

Figure 5.1. Regression Residuals and Error Terms for a Bivariate Regression Model
NOTE: e_j is the regression residual for observation j; ε_j is the error term.

where $\hat{Y}_j$ denotes the predicted Y value for the case based on the sample coefficient estimates. In the context of a graph of the *estimated* sample regression surface in which Y is measured on the vertical axis, the residual for a case, e_j, represents the vertical distance between this estimated regression surface and the observed value of Y for the case. For a bivariate model, this distance is shown in Figure 5.1 for the observation with an X value of X_j. In contrast, the error term, ε_j, reflects the vertical distance between the unobserved *population* regression surface and the observed value of Y for the case (also illustrated in Figure 5.1 for the bivariate case). It is essential to recognize that empirical analysis of the relationship between an independent variable and the OLS regression residuals for a sample *cannot* be used to assess whether an assumption that the independent variable is uncorrelated with the error term (A5 in the list in Chapter 2) is justified. This is because the least squares criterion ensures that regression residuals will always be completely uncorrelated with all independent variables, regardless of the distribution of the error term, ε.

To understand the substantive meaning of the assumption that the error term is uncorrelated with each independent variable (A5), we return to the conception of the error term—reflected in Equation 2.8— as representing the combined effect of all variables that influence the dependent variable but are excluded from the regression, along with any random component in the dependent variable's behavior. Formally, we can write

$$\varepsilon_j = \delta_0 + \delta_1 Z_{1j} + \delta_2 Z_{2j} + \ldots + \delta_m Z_{mj} + R_j, \qquad [5.3]$$

where the excluded independent variables are labeled as Zs, R denotes the random component, and the intercept of Equation 2.8 has been renamed δ_0. Given this conception of ε, the assumption that the error term is uncorrelated with each independent variable requires that $\sum_{i=1}^{m} \delta_i Z_{ij}$ be uncorrelated with each and every included X variable.[20] Although it is possible for the linear combination of the excluded explanatory variables (i.e., $\sum_{i=1}^{m} \delta_i Z_{ij}$) to be uncorrelated with each independent variable even when the individual Zs are not, the more confident one is, based on theory, that the excluded variables with the strongest effects on Y are at most weakly correlated with the included variables, the more confident one can be that assumption A5 is reasonable.

One situation in which the assumption that the error term is uncorrelated with each of the independent variables in a regression equation is guaranteed to be violated is when there is *reciprocal* causation, that is, when the dependent variable influences one or more of the independent variables. For instance, assume that

$$Y_j = \alpha + \beta_1 X_{1j} + \beta_2 X_{2j} + \ldots + \beta_k X_{kj} + \varepsilon_j, \qquad [5.4]$$

where all Gauss-Markov assumptions are met, except that no presumption is made about $\text{COV}(X_{1j}, \varepsilon_j)$. But suppose Y is a cause of X_1. For specificity, assume

$$X_{1j} = \alpha^* + \beta^* Y_j + u_j, \qquad [5.5]$$

where $\beta^* \neq 0$ and u is an error term. In this case, $\text{COV}(X_{1j}, \varepsilon_j)$ is bound to be different from zero. In essence, because ε is an error term influencing Y, when Y in turn influences X_1, ε is an "indirect" cause of X_1, and consequently, X_1 and ε must be correlated.[21] (A formal proof that when Y is a cause of X_1, $\text{COV}[X_{1j}, \varepsilon_j] \neq 0$ requires extensive mathematical manipulation; see Gujarati, 1988, pp. 563-564, for a proof in the case of a similar model.)

Specification Error:
Using the Wrong Independent Variables

In the most general sense, a *specification error* can be said to occur when a regression equation or one of its assumptions is incorrect in any way, but most social scientists use the term more narrowly to refer to mistakes in the way variables are incorporated into a regression model. A later section of this chapter—on the linearity and additivity assumptions—considers a type of specification error in which the "correct" variables are included, but the model inaccurately reflects the functional (or mathematical) form of the relationships among variables. The subject of this section is specification errors that occur when a regression equation is estimated with the "wrong" independent variables: Relevant variables are excluded, irrelevant variables are included, or both.

The very notions of "excluding relevant variables" and "including irrelevant variables" presume a criterion for judging the relevance of a variable to a model. Discussions of specification error in the literature typically propose one of two *frames of reference* for evaluating relevance: (a) a *true model* (discussed in Chapter 2) or (b) the *theory* motivating a regression. With the former, one judges a regression model by how well it conforms to the true model explaining a dependent variable. With the latter, a user of regression is presumed to have a theory, and the accuracy of the specification is judged by how well the regression model reflects the underlying theory. *My view is that a theory is a more sensible frame of reference for judging model specification than an elusive "true model."*

First, as we have seen, some challenge the notion that there is a unique true model to explain any given dependent variable. Second, even if we accept the presumption that a true model exists, the complete set of variables in it is inherently unknowable. Thus, in practice, it is virtually inconceivable that a true model could provide a unique concrete frame of reference to which an estimation regression model can be compared.

The alternative—treating a theory as the frame of reference—does have its dangers. Foremost, it may create a temptation to "work backwards": to begin by designing a regression model that includes only variables that can be measured in the available sample, and finish by "molding" a theory that includes precisely those variables. Such a strategy would guarantee the *nominal* absence of specification error, but the absence would be completely superficial. Consequently, any time we establish a theory as the appropriate frame of reference for analyzing the adequacy of a regression model, it is essential that we take very seriously criticism that the theory fails to take into account certain variables or specifies relationships in the wrong functional form. However, assuming that a researcher has given careful attention to theory construction, is satisfied that the resulting theory is sound, and has resisted making modifications in the theory based on anticipated data problems, the theory represents the most appropriate frame of reference for judging an estimation model.

Thus in this monograph I restrict the conception of a specification error of exclusion to the case in which one or more explanatory variables included in a *theory* are excluded from an *estimation model*. In analyzing the consequences of such an error, the strategy will be to assume we have a theory formalized as a regression equation. For example:

$$Y_j = \alpha + \beta_1 X_{1j} + \beta_2 X_{2j} + \beta_3 X_{3j} + \beta_4 X_{4j} + \beta_5 X_{5j} + \beta_6 X_{6j} + \varepsilon_j . \quad [5.6]$$
[the theory, formalized]

This equation contains a disturbance term, ε, that represents all those factors affecting Y that are not explicitly identified by the theory, along with any intrinsically random element in the behavior of Y. We assume that Equation 5.6 satisfies the Gauss-Markov assumptions. In essence, this assumption implies that the theory accurately represents the process by which Y is determined. If data were available to estimate the equation directly (so that the estimation model were identical to the theory), we would be assured that the OLS estimators were unbiased. But, instead, we will establish this equation as the frame of reference, assume that the estimation model excludes one or more of the Xs, and assess the consequences. For instance, assume that X_1 and X_2 are excluded, yielding

$$Y_j = \alpha + \beta_3 X_{3j} + \beta_4 X_{4j} + \beta_5 X_{5j} + \beta_6 X_{6j} + u_j , \quad [5.7]$$
[estimation model]

where the error term for the estimation equation is denoted u to distinguish it from the theory's ε.

The key to understanding the implications of this type of exclusion is to recognize that Equation 5.7 does not totally ignore the effects of X_1 and X_2 on Y; it just relegates those effects to the equation's error term. Put differently, u is a function both of ε and of X_1 and X_2:

$$u_j = \varepsilon_j + \beta_1 X_{1j} + \beta_2 X_{2j}.$$

And whereas ε is presumed to be *uncorrelated* with each of X_3, X_4, X_5, and X_6 (assumption A5), unless both X_1 and X_2 are uncorrelated with the other independent variables, u must be assumed to be *correlated* with X_3, X_4, X_5, and X_6, in violation of assumption A5. Thus understanding the consequences of a specification error of *exclusion* is the same as understanding the effects of violating the assumption that the error term is uncorrelated with each of the independent variables. However, it is very important to recognize that all the consequences of specification errors to be presented below rest on a presumption that the frame of reference model (i.e., the theory) satisfies the Gauss-Markov assumptions. For example, we shall see that if both X_1 and X_2 are uncorrelated with each of X_3, X_4, X_5, and X_6, in spite of the specification error, OLS estimators of the partial slope coefficients of Equation 5.7 are unbiased; but this lack of bias is contingent on the "truth" of the theory (i.e., on Equation 5.6 satisfying the Gauss-Markov assumptions).

At this point, we investigate more specifically the implications of a specification error of exclusion, beginning with the simplest case. The reference model contains two independent variables,

$$Y_j = \alpha + \beta_1 X_{1j} + \beta_2 X_{2j} + \varepsilon_j, \qquad \text{[frame of reference]}$$

and the estimation model excludes one of them:

$$Y_j = \alpha + \beta_1 X_{1j} + u_j. \qquad \text{[estimation model]}$$

We assume that the reference model satisfies the Gauss-Markov assumptions, that both β_1 and β_2 are greater than zero, and that X_1 and X_2 are positively correlated in the estimation sample. Intuition suggests that because (a) X_2 is excluded from the estimation regression and (b) X_1 and X_2 are positively correlated, some of X_2s positive influence on Y will be attributed to X_1, resulting in a tendency to overestimate the impact of X_1 on Y. This intuition proves correct. When X_2 is omitted, the estimator for β_1 is *positively biased*, with the magnitude of the bias determined by the strength of the effect of X_2 on Y in the population, and the strength of the relationship between X_1 and X_2 in the sample. In particular, $E(b_1) = \beta_1 + b_{21}\beta_2$, where b_{21} is the slope coefficient from what is called an *auxiliary regression*—specifically, the regression of X_2 on X_1 in the sample. If the correlation between X_1 and X_2 is positive, so too is b_{21}. Given that $\beta_2 > 0$, the product $b_{21}\beta_2 > 0$, confirming that the bias in b_1 is positive.

The implications of a specification error of exclusion can be stated precisely for the general case as well, as long as the reference model satisfies the Gauss-Markov assumptions (Deegan, 1976; Maddala, 1992, pp. 162-163; Rao & Miller, 1971).[22] Assume that the frame of reference model contains r variables $(X_1, X_2, \ldots, X_r)$ but that the estimation model includes only the first g of these. The bias in the OLS estimator for any included variable X_i $(1 \leq i \leq g)$ is given by the formula

$$E(b_i) = \beta_i + \sum_{j=g+1}^{r} b_{ji}\beta_j, \qquad [5.8]$$

where b_{ji} is the partial slope coefficient for X_i from the auxiliary regression of X_j on all g included variables $(X_1, X_2, \ldots, X_g)$. Thus the bias in b_i is a *weighted sum* of the partial slope coefficients for the excluded variables $(\beta_{g+1}, \beta_{g+2}, \ldots, \beta_r)$, where the weight for each β_j (i.e., b_{ji}) is a measure—derived from an auxiliary regression—of the strength of the relationship between X_j and X_i when all other included variables are held constant.

I will illustrate the meaning and implications of a specification error of exclusion with a "weight" example. Assume that we were to leave metabolic rate (METABOLISM) out of Equation 3.1 (being unable to measure it for individuals in a sample). Then, the error term for the incorrectly specified regression would be $u_j = \varepsilon_j - 1.795$ (METABOLISM$_j$). The ε component of this error term is uncorrelated with each of the independent variables in the model (assumption A5), but is METABOLISM? In practical research situations we could speculate, but we would not know for sure. However, in our contrived case the correlations between all pairs of variables are known and presented in Table 5.1. Note that METABOLISM is not highly correlated with the remaining independent variables; its bivariate correlation with other variables ranges from a magnitude of .32 (CALORIES and AGE) to virtually zero. Furthermore, when METABOLISM is regressed on all other independent variables in Equation 3.1, the resulting R^2 is only .31 (see Column 10). Most analysts would probably conclude that METABOLISM is not strongly collinear with the remaining independent variables.

Nevertheless, excluding METABOLISM from the set of regressors leads to substantial bias in some coefficient estimators. Column 2 of

TABLE 5.1
Relationships Among Independent Variables in Equation 3.1
in Population of 134 Women

	(1) CALORIES	(2) FAT	(3) EXERCISE	(4) HEIGHT	(5) AGE	(6) SMOKER	(7) F^2 FAT	(8) SMOKER · EXERCISE	(9) METABOLISM	(10) R^2
CALORIES	1.00									.66
FAT	.78	1.00								.97
EXERCISE	−.35	−.25	1.00							.41
HEIGHT	.25	.24	−.31	1.00						.16
AGE	.27	.30	−.25	.09	1.00					.35
SMOKER	.29	.35	−.06	.06	.27	1.00				.37
FAT²	.77	.98	−.22	.23	.33	.37	1.00			.97
SMOKER · EXERCISE	.10	.17	.34	.03	.12	.49	.18	1.00		.41
METABOLISM	.32	.25	.00	.18	−.32	.08	.24	.03	1.00	.31

NOTE: Values in Columns 1 through 9 are bivariate correlations; values in Column 10 are R^2 values when the variable in the left margin is regressed on the remaining independent variables in Equation 3.1.

Table 5.2 shows the expected value of parameter estimators for Equation 3.1 when METABOLISM is excluded.[23] Column 3 gives a measure of "relative" estimator bias; it presents the ratio of the difference between the expected value of the estimator with METABOLISM excluded and the expected value with no specification error to the expected value with no error. The specification bias is most serious in the case of the age variable, as the expected value of b_A reverses sign. The true effect is one in which an additional decade of age is associated with an average weight reduction of 2.85 pounds, but the misspecified model indicates that as age increases by 10 years, expected weight *increases* by 1.90 pounds. In addition, three other partial slope coefficient estimators are biased by more than 30% in the direction of weaker magnitudes—those for CALORIES, HEIGHT, and SMOKER.

Good example

TABLE 5.2
Illustration of Effects of Specification Error:
Excluding Variables From Equation 3.1

Variable	Parameter	(1) Population Value (Without Specification Error)[a]	(2) Excluding METABOLISM — Expected Value of Parameter Estimator With Specification Error	(3) Excluding METABOLISM — Percentage Bias as a Result of Specification Error[b]	(4) Excluding METABOLISM and FAT — Expected Value of Parameter Estimator With Specification Error	(5) Excluding METABOLISM and FAT — Percentage Bias as a Result of Specification Error[c]
Intercept	α	38.10	65.83	0.73	−26.84	−1.70
CALORIES	β_C	0.0291	0.0199	−0.32	0.0424	0.46
FAT	β_F	−3.098	−3.001	−0.03	—	—
EXERCISE	β_E	−0.1183	−0.1384	0.17	−0.0854	−0.28
HEIGHT	β_H	1.346	0.817	−0.39	1.154	−0.14
AGE	β_A	−0.285	0.190	−1.66	0.418	−2.47
SMOKER	β_S	3.01	1.46	−0.51	5.43	0.78
FAT^2	β_{FF}	0.084	0.080	−0.05	—	—
SMOKER • EXERCISE	β_{SE}	0.1097	0.1299	0.18	.1033	−0.06
METABOLISM	β_M	−1.795	—	—	—	—

NOTES: a. As presented in the text.
b. (Value in Column 2 − value in Column 1)/value in Column 1.
c. (Value in Column 4 − value in Column 1)/value in Column 1.

Formula 5.8 tells us that to learn the exact amount of bias resulting from a specification error of exclusion, we would need to know (a) the partial slope coefficient (in the frame of reference equation) for each excluded variable and (b) the partial slope coefficients from the auxiliary regressions of each of the excluded variables on all included variables. In practice, the former coefficients—being population values—are intrinsically unknowable, and the latter coefficients could not be calculated without data for the excluded variables. However, when only a single independent variable is excluded, the amount of bias ($\sum b_{ji}\beta_j$ in Formula 5.8) simplifies to a single product, and the theory motivating the regression analysis will sometimes allow reasonable inferences about the sign of this product: positive or negative. For instance, assume an analyst is concerned about the effect of excluding X_2 on the partial coefficient estimator b_1 in some model. The logic underlying the theory should yield a prediction about the sign of β_2. In many situations, the analyst will also have some information or, at least, some intuition about the sign of the slope coefficient (b_{21}) for X_1 in the auxiliary regression of X_2 on all included variables. Perhaps the relationship between X_1 and X_2 has been investigated in another study, so that empirical support for a proposition about the sign of b_{21} is available. In other situations, a researcher would be forced to rely on "informed speculation" about the sign of the bivariate correlation between X_1 and X_2. In turn, these predictions about the signs of β_2 and b_{21} lead to a clear prediction about the direction of the bias, since the bias is the product of these two values.

Let us assume that we did not know the population parameters for Equation 3.1, and that although our theory leads us to believe that metabolic rate influences a person's weight, lack of data forces us to exclude METABOLISM from the estimation equation. What kinds of inferences could we reasonably make about the bias produced in parameter estimators as a result of the specification error?[24] If we have no a priori theory (or even intuition) about the sign of the relationship between METABOLISM and a particular independent variable controlling for the remaining independent variables, the direction of the bias in the coefficient estimator for that independent variable cannot be predicted.

But in some cases, we could make a reasonable prediction about the likely direction of bias. For example, consider the parameter for food intake (CALORIES), β_C. Using Formula 5.8, and treating METABOLISM as the single excluded variable, we get

$$E(b_C) = \beta_C + b_{MC}\beta_M, \qquad [5.9]$$

where b_{MC} is the partial slope coefficient for CALORIES in the auxiliary regression of METABOLISM on all independent variables in Equation 3.1 (except METABOLISM). Assume that our theory proposes that β_M is negative, based on a belief that an increase in metabolic rate should cause a decrease in weight. If we are prepared to assume that b_{MC} is positive, based on an impression that persons with faster metabolisms tend to eat more, then we could conclude that $b_{MC}\beta_M$ is negative. Formula 5.9 would then imply that an estimate of β_C based on a regression excluding METABOLISM tends to be "too negative," that is, to be equal to the true parameter, β_C, plus a negative number. How useful this information is depends upon the sign of the estimate for β_C in a particular sample. If b_C is negative, the information that this estimate is probably "too negative" leaves us uncertain about the likely sign of the true parameter, which could be "less negative" (but still negative) or positive. If, as is more likely, b_C is positive in some sample, the information that this estimate is probably "too negative" would allow us to conclude that our estimate likely *under*estimates the strength of the positive relationship between food intake and weight.

When two or more independent variables in a frame of reference model are excluded from an estimation regression, the directions of the resulting bias in partial slope coefficient estimators are more difficult to predict. Note that in such a case, the bias in an estimator is a weighted sum of the partial slope coefficients for the excluded variables, where the weights are positive or negative depending on the nature of the relationships between excluded and included variables in the sample. Thus the first step in predicting the direction of bias is to predict the sign of each of the $r - g$ products of a slope coefficient (β_j) and a weight (b_{ji}) in the summation term of Formula 5.8. Only in the unusual circumstance that *all* $r - g$ products in the sum are predicted to be positive, or *all* are predicted to be negative, will an analyst likely be able to make a clear prediction about the direction of bias. If, instead, some of these products are thought to be positive and some are predicted to be negative, unless one can go beyond predictions of the signs of these products to predictions about *specific* values, it will be unclear whether (a) the positive products will "cancel out" the negative products in the sum to yield near-zero bias, or (b) the positive (or negative) products will dominate the sum to produce a large positive (or negative) bias.

As an illustration of the "unpredictability" of the direction and magnitude of bias when more than one regressor is excluded, we can compare the bias produced by deleting both FAT and METABOLISM from Equation 3.1 to that when just METABOLISM is omitted. Table 5.2 provides the comparisons. When we exclude FAT as well as METABOLISM, the bias in the coefficient estimator for AGE becomes even more pronounced. But this is not true for all coefficients; for instance, the bias in the estimator for HEIGHT is lessened. And the change in the pattern of bias follows no obvious pattern either. The coefficient estimator for EXERCISE that tended to be *over*estimated in magnitude is now *under*estimated, and the estimator for SMOKER that was substantially *under*estimated is now appreciably *over*estimated.

This discussion of specification error suggests a research strategy in which an assessment of the implications of such error becomes an integral part of regression analysis. The first steps are the development of a theory and its "translation" into the form of a regression equation. If the analyst believes this equation satisfies the Gauss-Markov assumptions, it can be conceived as a *frame of reference* for evaluating an estimation model. If the analyst is *very* lucky, all variables in the frame of reference model can be observed in the sample, and the reference equation is "short" enough—given the sample size—to avoid severe multicollinearity. Then model estimation can proceed free of specification errors. But in the more typical case, data for some variables in the reference equation will be unavailable, or that model will be too "long," and thus estimation will require errors of exclusion. A tempting response to the prospect that specification errors will be necessary is to skip the stage of theory construction, or at least "blend it in" with the estimation stage, by taking into account data availability and likely sources of multicollinearity when simultaneously developing a theory and a perfectly matching regression model. But if theory construction and specification of the estimation model become a single process, the possibility of assessing the impact of exclusions made necessary by estimation problems is sacrificed unnecessarily.

The appropriate research strategy is considered below in three situations in which the estimation regression excludes independent variables from the frame of reference equation: (a) when one or more specific independent variables cannot be observed in the estimation sample, (b) when all independent variables are inherently observable but limits on time and resources make it infeasible to collect data for all these variables, and (c) when estimating the full frame of reference model would result in severe multicollinearity.

When an inability to observe specific variables in a sample forces the exclusion of these variables, if theory or empirical evidence from other samples gives us confidence that each of the excluded variables are at most weakly correlated with each of the included variables, we can be confident that the exclusions will not result in substantial bias in the coefficient estimators for included variables. If there are substantial correlations between included and excluded independent variables, coefficient estimators may be heavily biased. The only question is whether we can say something about the direction of the bias. We saw above that if just one or two variables are excluded, it may be possible to draw reasonable inferences about the sign of the resulting bias. But if many variables are unobservable, it will be very unlikely that the direction of the bias can be identified.

What if the problem is lack of resources? Each variable in the reference equation is potentially measurable, but it is impractical to collect data for the full set of independent variables. Here an understanding of the consequences of specification error provides a reasonable criterion for deciding which independent variables to exclude. Often, when a researcher is asked to identify the purpose of a research project relying on regression analysis, he or she will speak of developing a *complete* or *comprehensive* explanation of some dependent variable. Taken literally, such a goal is tantamount to finding the "true model," an objective that is, for all practical purposes, unattainable. But usually, when pressed for more specificity about the purpose of research, the analyst will begin speaking of a research question that focuses attention on one independent variable, or a relatively small set of independent variables. Thus, although the frame of reference model may contain numerous independent variables, the researcher will typically be interested primarily in the effects of a small subset that we might call the *core variables*. If the researcher could obtain unbiased and precise estimates of the coefficients for these core variables, he or she would be quite pleased. This suggests that if time or financial constraints limit the number of variables that can be included in a regression, the goal should be to include the core variables, and to add to these the subset of independent variables from the frame of reference model that would maximize our ability to get "good" estimates of the slope coefficients for the core variables, subject to the constraints on data collection. This implies that the variables most important to include in the estimation regression are those that are highly correlated with the core variables in the sample; those safest to exclude are ones that are only weakly correlated with each of the core variables. Of course, we will not know the values of these correlations in the sample. But information about the relationships among the variables in other samples, or theory—or both—might serve as a basis for a reasonable choice about what to exclude.

A final possibility is that, if there are (a) few enough cases in the estimation sample, (b) a large enough number of independent variables in the reference model, and/or (c) high enough correlations among these independent variables, the reference equation may be characterized by severe multicollinearity. Because multicollinearity is at root a problem of insufficient information in the sample, the only fully satisfactory solution for overcoming the problem is more data. Increasing the sample size will always improve the efficiency of coefficient estimators, as long as (a) the additional cases have independent variable values different from the mean values of the variables in the sample, and (b) these cases do not serve to increase the correlations among the independent variables (Kmenta, 1986, pp. 439-440).

Barring the availability of more data, if one is confident enough to make assumptions about the values of some of the parameters of the reference model (based on theory or empirical evidence from other samples), such "knowledge" can be used to obtain more efficient estimators of coefficients than would be possible if the data had to be used to estimate *all* parameters.[25] If prior knowledge cannot be tapped, severe collinearity may make accepting some bias—by excluding one or more independent variables—to gain precision in estimators an attractive trade-off. However, when multicollinearity (and not an inability to observe variables) is the reason for exclusion, one need not speculate about the specification bias introduced; one can undertake direct empirical analysis of the consequences of variable exclusion by conducting a *sensitivity analysis*. This approach involves (a) estimating coefficients for the "full" reference model (which yields *unbiased* estimators with *large* standard errors) and a variety of inaccurately specified "submodels," each of which includes the core variables but excludes a different combination of independent variables (thereby yielding *biased* estimators with *smaller* standard errors), and (b) assessing the stability of coefficient estimates for the core variables across the multiple estimations. For example, assume (a) the theory predicts that β_1 is positive; (b) the point estimate for β_1 is consistently positive for both the "full" reference model and a variety of misspecified submodels, ranging in value from a low of b_1^L to a high of b_1^H; and (c) an increase of even b_1^L in the dependent variable resulting from a unit increase in X_1 is viewed as indicative of a strong effect. Under these conditions, even if the confidence interval for β_1 based on the estimate from the full model includes zero, it seems appropriate to reject the null hypothesis that $\beta_1 = 0$ in favor of the research hypothesis that $\beta_1 > 0$. In contrast, if the different submodels yield estimates of β_1 with widely varying magnitudes, there is little alternative to accepting the conclusion that, given the data available, there is simply no way to obtain precise estimates of the individual effects of the core variables in the theory.

To conclude this section, I should note that the entire discussion of specification error thus far rests on the assumption that there *is* a clear reference model, so that the estimation model can be compared with the frame of reference to analyze the implications of using the "wrong" model in empirical research. When an investigator has two or more competing theories of a phenomenon, and the goal of empirical analysis is to determine which theory is true, the approach I present for analyzing the effects of specification errors is of little help. An alternative strategy involves estimating a "nested" model. For example, if there are two competing models, I and II, to explain a dependent variable Y,

$$Y_j = \delta_0 + \delta_1 X_{1j} + \delta_2 X_{2j} + \varepsilon_{1j}, \qquad \text{[Model I]}$$

and

$$Y_j = \mu_0 + \mu_3 X_{3j} + \mu_4 X_{4j} + \varepsilon_{2j}, \qquad \text{[Model II]}$$

one would estimate the coefficients of the nested model that includes the independent variables from both Model I and Model II:

$$Y_j = \beta_0 + \beta_1 X_{1j} + \beta_2 X_{2j} + \beta_3 X_{3j} + \beta_4 X_{4j} + \varepsilon_j. \qquad [5.10]$$

Then, if the estimates for β_1 and β_2 are statistically significant, and those for β_3 and β_4 are not, a reasonable inference is that Model I is true. Similarly, if b_3 and b_4 are significant, but b_1 and b_2 are not, Model II would be presumed correct. One potential fly in the ointment in this approach is substantial multicollinearity among the four Xs, because such multicollinearity would make it likely that none of the partial slope coefficient estimates for Equation 5.10 would be significant even if one of the models were correct.[26]

The Assumption That the Mean of the Error Term Is Zero

Among the assumptions of the standard regression model is that the disturbance term has a zero mean (A4 in Chapter 2). Formally, it is assumed that in the equation

$$Y_j = \alpha + \beta_1 X_{1j} + \beta_2 X_{2j} + \ldots + \beta_k X_{kj} + \varepsilon_j,$$

$E(\varepsilon_j | X_{1j}, X_{2j}, \ldots, X_{kj}) = 0$. If this assumption is violated, then $E(\varepsilon_j | X_{1j}, X_{2j}, \ldots, X_{kj}) = \mu_j$, where μ_j is not uniformly zero. Then, it is no longer the case that

$$E(Y_j | X_{1j}, X_{2j}, \ldots, X_{kj}) = \alpha + \beta_1 X_{1j} + \beta_2 X_{2j} + \ldots + \beta_k X_{kj}. \quad [5.11]$$

Instead,

$$E(Y_j | X_{1j}, X_{2j}, \ldots, X_{kj}) = \alpha + \beta_1 X_{1j} + \beta_2 X_{2j} + \ldots + \beta_k X_{kj} + \mu_j. \quad [5.12]$$

There are two possibilities: Either (a) μ_j is constant across observations or (b) μ_j varies. The latter has more serious consequences.

First, consider the case where μ_j is constant, so that for all observations, $\mu_j = \mu$. It can be shown that as long as the remaining Gauss-Markov assumptions are satisfied, the least squares estimators of partial slope coefficients remain unbiased. The OLS *intercept* estimator, however, is biased by μ units. We can confirm this by fixing μ_j in Equation 5.12 at the constant, μ, and rearranging terms to yield

$$E(Y_j | X_{1j}, X_{2j}, \ldots, X_{kj}) = (\alpha + \mu) + \beta_1 X_{1j} + \beta_2 X_{2j} + \ldots + \beta_k X_{kj}.$$

Clearly, if OLS were used with this equation, the intercept estimator would be estimating $\alpha + \mu$ instead of α, and therefore would be producing an estimator of α biased by μ units.

Measurement error in a dependent variable in which each observation's score is uniformly "off" by a fixed absolute amount will produce an error term with a nonzero, but constant, mean. For instance, assume that the weights of a sample of women from our illustrative population had been determined by a single "doctor's" scale that undermeasured all weights by 5 pounds. In this case, the estimation equation would not be Equation 3.1, but instead

$$(\text{WEIGHT}_j - 5) = \alpha + \beta_C \text{CALORIES}_j + \beta_F \text{FAT}_j + \beta_E \text{EXERCISE}_j + \ldots + \varepsilon_{Wj}.$$

Adding 5 to both sides of this equation yields an equivalent equation,

$$\text{WEIGHT}_j = \alpha + \beta_C \text{CALORIES}_j + \beta_F \text{FAT}_j + \beta_E \text{EXERCISE}_j + \ldots + (5 + \varepsilon_{Wj}),$$

having an error term with mean 5.

What about the case when the mean of the error term, μ_j, varies across observations? In the standard regression model—with all Gauss-Markov assumptions satisfied—the expected value of the dependent variable is determined exclusively by the parameters (α, β_1, β_2, . . .) and the values of the independent variables, as in Equation 5.11. But when the mean of the disturbance term varies across cases, the expected value of Y is determined by the regression parameters, the values of the Xs, *and* μ (as in Equation 5.12). In effect, μ becomes a relevant variable that is excluded from the regression equation, resulting in bias in the partial slope coefficient estimators.

Indeed, in general, a specification error of exclusion results in an error term the value of which varies across observations. Specifically, this occurs when at least one of the excluded variables is correlated with at least one of the included independent variables. In contrast, when *all* excluded variables are uncorrelated with each included variable, the mean of the error term is constant but nonzero.[27]

The disturbance term of a regression equation will also have a varying mean when there is a *truncated* sample, that is, when analysis is restricted to cases having an observed score either (a) greater than some fixed value or (b) less than some fixed value. As an illustration, assume we consider only those women in our example who weigh less than 150 pounds. For simplicity, we examine a bivariate model in which, *in the full population*, a woman's weight is determined by her height and an error term:[28]

$$\text{WEIGHT}_j = \alpha + \beta\text{HEIGHT}_j + \varepsilon_j, \qquad [5.13]$$

where the Gauss-Markov assumptions are presumed to be satisfied. This population regression equation is graphed as the solid line in Figure 5.2. The dots and x's (together) represent a hypothetical random sample from the full population of women, with dots denoting observations for women weighing less than 150 pounds and x's denoting observations for women weighing more than 150.

Among women *weighing less than 150 pounds*, the expected value of the error term is negatively related to the independent variable, HEIGHT. To see why this is so, consider first the value of HEIGHT for which the expected value of WEIGHT is 150; this value is labeled H^* in Figure 5.2. For a case for which HEIGHT = H^* to be in the restricted population, the error term ε must be negative or zero; if ε were positive, then WEIGHT for the case would be greater than 150. Consequently, at H^*, $E(\varepsilon_j | \text{HEIGHT}_j)$ must be negative. Next, consider a value of HEIGHT, H', just slightly less than H^*. At H', to be in the restricted population, ε must be negative, zero, or slightly positive, thereby making $E(\varepsilon_j | \text{HEIGHT}_j)$

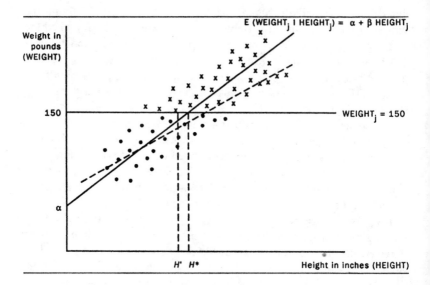

Figure 5.2. Illustration of a Violation of the Assumption That the Expected Value of the Error Term Is Zero

less negative than at H^*. Indeed, at any height value less than H^*, the maximum positive value of ε is equal to the vertical distance between the regression line and the horizontal line (WEIGHT$_j$ = 150) in Figure 5.2. Because this maximum value for ε gets larger as HEIGHT decreases, $E(\varepsilon_j|\text{HEIGHT}_j)$ remains negative, but approaches zero as HEIGHT decreases. Therefore, in the population of women less than 150 pounds, $E(\varepsilon_j|\text{HEIGHT}_j)$ is negatively correlated with the independent variable HEIGHT$_j$, making the OLS estimator for β biased. It is clear from Figure 5.2 that the estimated regression line based on the sample of cases from the restricted population would underestimate the true population slope, as the line best fitting just the dots (and not the x's)—denoted by dashes—is flatter than the population line.

This underestimation of the slope coefficient in the weight example reflects the typical case. In most applications, if the population model

$$Y_j = \alpha + \beta X_j + \varepsilon_j$$

were estimated with a sample restricted to observations from either (a) the population of cases for which Y_j is greater than some constant or (b) the population of cases for which Y_j is less than a constant, the slope coefficient estimator would be biased toward zero, that is, $|E(b)| < |\beta|$.[29] Estimation with a sample restricted in this fashion can be viewed as one form of *selection bias*. Selection bias occurs when a sample from a population under- or overrepresents one or more types of cases. In the example based on Equation 5.13, light persons are overrepresented. A similar form of selection bias might characterize bivariate regression analysis of the effect of education on annual earnings. Using typical data sources, the estimation of this model is likely to be based on a sample restricted to individuals who are employed. By excluding all *un*employed individuals, who have zero income, the slope coefficient estimator would tend to underestimate the strength of the relationship between education and earnings in the general population.

Of course, other forms of selection bias are possible. In the previous examples, the probability that an observation is included in the estimation sample is determined by the observation's value on the dependent variable. In other situations, the probability that an observation is included may be a function of other variables. And in general, when there is selection bias, slope coefficient estimators will be biased unless the variables determining the probability of the inclusion of a case in the sample are uncorrelated with each of the independent variables. For example, assume Equation 3.1 (the weight model) is estimated for a sample composed of volunteers (or self-selectors) recruited using notices posted in residential neighborhoods on telephone poles, and the notices are placed so that women with odd-numbered street addresses are more likely to see the signs than those with even-numbered addresses. In this case, the probability of a woman being included in the sample should be a function of whether her address is odd or even. But it is reasonable to assume that whether one's street address is even or odd is uncorrelated with each of the independent variables in Equation 3.1. Consequently, the selection bias should not produce bias in slope coefficient estimators. In contrast, if the sample for estimation were self-selected, and older women (perhaps having more free time) were more likely to volunteer for participation than younger women, slope coefficient estimators would be biased.

Assumptions About Level of Measurement

Assumption A1 requires that the independent variables in a regression be quantitative or dichotomous, and that the dependent variable be quantitative, continuous, and unbounded.[30] In the regression model, an

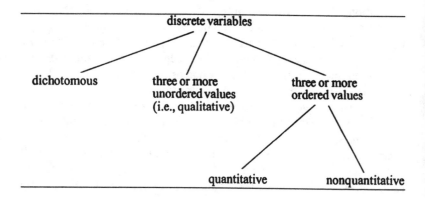

Figure 5.3. Differences in Types of Discrete Variables

observation's value on the dependent variable is assumed to be a function of the value of each of the independent variables, the parameters (i.e., α and the β_is), and the value of the error term. Thus the dependent variable must be free to take on any numerical value that this function yields. This is why the assumption of a continuous unbounded dependent variable is required.[31] Strictly speaking, no variables used in practice are completely continuous. Even an object's "length," which if it could be measured *exactly* would undoubtedly be continuous, is only approximately continuous when observed with imperfect precision (e.g., to the nearest tenth of an inch).[32] And although there is no firm guideline on how close a variable must be to continuous for the assumption to be met approximately, some variables, such as the net worth of an individual measured to the nearest dollar, are clearly close enough.

There are a variety of types of discrete (i.e., noncontinuous) variables, some of which are appropriate in a regression model, others of which are not. Figure 5.3 summarizes the differences in types. Discrete variables can (a) be dichotomous, (b) *qualitative*[33]—that is, have three or more values that are *unordered* (e.g., an individual's race, measured in five categories as Asian, African American, Hispanic, Caucasian, or other)—or (c) have three or more values that are *ordered* (e.g., the number of children in a household or the number of candidates running in a primary election).[34] In turn, within the category of ordered discrete variables, we can distinguish those that are quantitative from those that are not.

To be appropriate as independent variables in a regression model, ordered discrete variables must be quantitative. But whether an ordered discrete variable is quantitative is not always obvious. Certainly, the choice to label the values of such a variable with sequential integers does not necessarily make it quantitative. For example, one can label the values of an ordered discrete variable that can assume three values—low, medium, and high—1, 2, and 3. But the variable would be quantitative only if the *distance* between "low" and "medium" is identical to the distance between "medium" and "high," where "distance" refers to the difference in the amount of the property being measured. For instance, if religious tolerance is the property, the variable is quantitative only if the difference in degree of tolerance between high tolerance and medium tolerance is the same as the difference between medium and low tolerance.

Under certain conditions, it may also be appropriate to treat a quantitative ordered discrete variable as if it were continuous, thereby justifying its use as a dependent variable in a regression model. In particular, when a quantitative ordered discrete variable takes on a wide range of values (as does the number of employees in an organization), it is probably reasonable to treat the variable as if it were continuous. In contrast, it is clearly inappropriate to treat any ordered discrete variable with a small number of values (say, five or fewer) as continuous. In between these extremes the choice is less obvious, but, as a general guideline, the greater the number of values assumed by a quantitative ordered discrete variable, the more reasonable an assumption of approximate continuousness and the stronger the case that it is appropriate to employ the variable as a dependent variable in a regression model.

Qualitative (i.e., unordered discrete) variables and nonquantitative ordered discrete variables are never appropriate as distinct regressors in a regression model. Nevertheless, the influence on a dependent variable of either of these types of variables can be incorporated through the use of two or more dichotomous regressors, each of which indicates whether a case assumes a specified value. (For a discussion of the proper construction of these dichotomous regressors, see page 25; see also Gujarati, 1988, chap. 14; Johnson et al., 1987, pp. 182-192; Schroeder, Sjoquist, & Stephan, 1986, pp. 56-58.)[35]

The consequences of a dichotomous dependent variable for a regression are worth examining at some length. Consider the standard regression model (Equation 2.2), where Y can assume only the values 0 and 1.

Rewriting this equation so as to isolate the error term on the left side, we get

$$\varepsilon_j = Y_j - \left(\alpha + \sum_{i=1}^{k} \beta_i X_{ij}\right).$$

This expression for ε_j shows that if Y can take on only the values 1 and 0, then for each set of values for the Xs, ε_j can also take on only two values: $1 - (\alpha + \sum_{i=1}^{k} \beta_i X_{ij})$ and $-(\alpha + \sum_{i=1}^{k} \beta_i X_{ij})$. The most obvious implication is that with a dichotomous Y, the assumption of a normally distributed error term is always violated. It can also be shown that the variance of the error term can be expressed as

$$\text{VAR}(\varepsilon_j | X_{1j}, X_{2j}, \ldots, X_{kj})$$

$$= E(Y_j | X_{1j}, X_{2j}, \ldots, X_{kj}) \cdot [1 - E(Y_j | X_{1j}, X_{2j}, \ldots, X_{kj})]$$

$$= (\alpha + \sum_{i=1}^{k} \beta_i X_{ij}) \cdot [1 - (\alpha + \sum_{i=1}^{k} \beta_i X_{ij})],$$

making it clear that the variance of the error term varies systematically with the values of the independent variables, and therefore that the homoscedasticity assumption is violated (Aldrich & Nelson, 1984, p. 13).

But the most serious problem with a regression involving a dichotomous dependent variable is the possibility of coefficients with "nonsensical" interpretations. In the case of a 0-1 dependent variable, the expected value of Y must equal (1 multiplied by the probability that Y equals 1) plus (0 multiplied by the probability that Y equals 0), or, in equation form,

$$E(Y_j | X_{1j}, X_{2j}, \ldots, X_{kj}) = [1 \cdot P(Y_j = 1 | X_{1j}, X_{2j}, \ldots, X_{kj})]$$
$$+ [0 \cdot P(Y_j = 0 | X_{1j}, X_{2j}, \ldots, X_{kj})]. \quad [5.14]$$

Because the rightmost bracketed term in this equation always equals 0, Equation 5.14 reduces to

$$E(Y_j | X_{1j}, X_{2j}, \ldots, X_{kj}) = P(Y_j = 1 | X_{1j}, X_{2j}, \ldots, X_{kj}),$$

implying that with a dependent variable that can equal only 0 or 1, the expected value of Y_j can be interpreted as the *probability* that Y_j equals 1.[36] But there is nothing that restricts $E(Y_j|X_{1j}, X_{2j}, \ldots, X_{kj}) = \alpha + \sum_{i=1}^{k} \beta_i X_{ij}$ to the range between 0 and 1. Therefore, the probability that Y_j equals 1 can take on nonsensical values less than 0 or greater than 1.

Furthermore, in most cases involving a dichotomous dependent variable, the linearity assumption of regression will not be plausible. The linearity assumption and the resulting unrestricted nature of the expected value of the dependent variable is reflected in the graph in Figure 5.4(a) for the bivariate case. In this case, the regression model's linearity assumption implies that even when $P(Y_j = 1|X_j)$ is .01 or .99, the effect of the independent variable on that probability is accurately reflected by the slope coefficient β. But in most situations, an assumption of a gradual decrease in the effect of independent variables as the probability that Y equals 1 approaches 0.00 or 1.00 would be more plausible. In such cases, the *non*linear specifications reflected in the *logit* or *probit* models would be preferable (see Aldrich & Nelson, 1984).[37] The latter specification is graphed in Figure 5.4(b) for the bivariate case, and the logit specification is quite similar in shape.

The Assumption of Measurement Without Error

To understand the substantive meaning of the regression assumption of *error-free* measurement, it is helpful to specify a formal measurement model. Most forms of measurement error can be conceived as situations in which a *true score* (or *concept*), T, is measured with an *indicator* (or *observed score*), I, where the observed score for any object, j, is a function, f, of both the true score and an error term, v:

$$I_j = f(T_j, v_j). \qquad [5.15]$$

How close one can hope to come to error-free measurement depends on the theoretical clarity of the concept. For example, it is certainly possible to conceive of measuring the true score of the variable "the percentage of the adult population in a state voting in the most recent presidential election" without appreciable error. But consider the concept "satisfaction with life" measured with an index constructed from survey items. With this variable, it is much more difficult to imagine measuring the true score exactly, because there is likely to be no clear

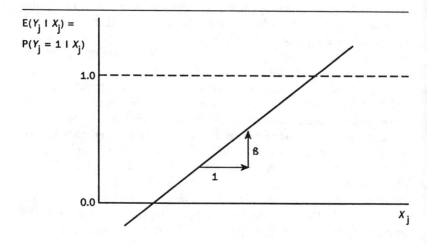

$E(Y_j \mid X_j) =$
$P(Y_j = 1 \mid X_j)$

1.0

β

1

0.0

X_j

(a) The Linear Model for a Single Independent Variable, X

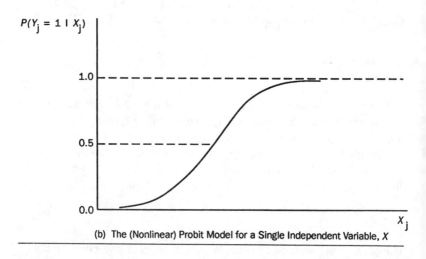

$P(Y_j = 1 \mid X_j)$

1.0

0.5

0.0

X_j

(b) The (Nonlinear) Probit Model for a Single Independent Variable, X

Figure 5.4. Bivariate Models With a Dichotomous Observed Dependent Variable

rule by which specific respondent choices on the items composing the index can be associated with precise absolute amounts of "satisfaction."

It is essential to distinguish several types of measurement error, each of which can be expected in different substantive situations. The first critical distinction is between *random* and *nonrandom* error.

RANDOM MEASUREMENT ERROR

The key requirement for measurement error to be conceived as *random* is for the error term to be unrelated to the true score (i.e., COV[T_j, v_j] = 0).[38] Errors that can occur in "transferring" data are the ones most likely to satisfy the assumption of randomness. Included would be errors made in recording data from documents on code sheets and errors in entering data from code sheets in a computer file. When data are collected from human respondents in surveys using closed-ended questions, any pure guessing by respondents would lead to random error; also, fatigue on the part of respondents should lead to such error. In a similar fashion, vagueness in the questions might lead to error that is largely random. However, it would be a mistake to conclude that all errors in survey responses are random, as any *systematic* bias in responses (e.g., the social pressure on individuals who failed to vote to report that they did, and the tendency of people to overreport their income and underreport their age) would lead to *non*random measurement error.

Random measurement error (RME) is least troublesome for regression analysis when it is confined to the dependent variable. In this situation, parameter estimators remain unbiased;[39] however, these estimators are less efficient, and R^2 values are attenuated (Berry & Feldman, 1985, p. 28; Johnson et al., 1987, pp. 327-329). When there is RME in an independent variable of a regression model, parameter estimators are biased, such that the amount of bias for an estimator is a function of the magnitude of the measurement error and the correlations among independent variables (Berry & Feldman, 1985, pp. 28-31). Only in the case of the *bivariate* model is the direction of the bias resulting from RME in an independent variable readily predictable; here, the expected value of the single slope coefficient estimator is always *smaller* in magnitude than its true population value (i.e., |E[b]| < |β|).[40]

NONRANDOM MEASUREMENT ERROR

Any measurement error not purely random in form is termed *nonrandom*. In contrast to the case of RME, nonrandom measurement error (NRME) will *always* lead to bias in OLS estimators. But the nature of the bias, and how pernicious it is, depends on the form of the error.

Within the class of nonrandom errors, Namboodiri, Carter, and Blalock (1975) distinguish broadly between (a) *errors that are a function of the variable being measured* and (b) *errors due to "extraneous" variables*. Even among errors that are a function of the variable being measured, there are a variety of types (Namboodiri et al., 1975, p. 575). In some cases, these errors can be conceived as *linear*:

- **Intercept errors:** $I_j = T_j + \delta$, where δ is a constant, so that across all observations, the indicator over- or underestimates the true score by a constant absolute amount.
- **Scale errors:** $I_j = \mu T_j$, where μ is a constant, so that the indicator over- or underestimates the true score by a constant percentage.
- **Both scale and intercept errors:** $I_j = \mu T_j + \delta$, where μ and δ are constants.

But in the more general case of error as a function of the variable being measured, the indicator can be *nonlinearly* related to the true score according to a variety of functional forms.

One needs to be concerned about the presence of an intercept measurement error only when one is substantively interested in the intercept (α) for the regression equation, because partial slope coefficient estimators and R^2 values are totally unaffected by such an error. Moreover, if the magnitude of an intercept error (i.e., the value of δ in the defining model) is known, an OLS intercept estimator can be corrected for bias due to measurement error. Assume, for instance, that the data used for estimating Equation 2.2 systematically overestimate some independent variable, X_1, by δ units. Then, although we believe that Equation 2.2 is being estimated,

$$Y_j = \alpha + \beta_1(X_{1j} + \delta) + \beta_2 X_{2j} + \ldots + \beta_k X_{kj} + \varepsilon_j$$

is actually being estimated. Multiplying out the term including X_1 gives

$$Y_j = \alpha + \beta_1 X_{1j} + \beta_1 \delta + \beta_2 X_{2j} + \ldots + \beta_k X_{kj} + \varepsilon_j.$$

Rearranging terms then yields

$$Y_j = (\alpha + \delta\beta_1) + \beta_1 X_{1j} + \beta_2 X_{2j} + \ldots + \beta_k X_{kj} + \varepsilon_j.$$

So to correct the original intercept estimate for the effect of NRME in this case, one would simply add to that estimate δ multiplied by the partial slope coefficient estimate for β_1. A similar analysis yields the correction factor when the *dependent* variable is measured with an intercept error. If the indicator for Y (in Equation 2.2) uniformly is δ units greater than the true score, the intercept estimate can be corrected for the effects of measurement error by subtracting δ.

We can also determine the procedures necessary for correcting for bias resulting from a *scale* error, if the magnitude of the error is known. If in lieu of the true score for the dependent variable, Y, one measures μY (where μ is a constant), the intercept estimate and all partial slope coefficient estimates will be inflated by a factor of μ, thereby requiring a correction by division of all these estimates by μ. For example, if the weights of women in our illustrative population were determined through surveys, and all women in the population underreported their true weight by 10%, then each of the parameter estimates would be biased downward, and the correct values could be calculated by dividing the original values by 0.90.[41] In contrast, if instead of measuring the true score for an independent variable, X_i, the indicator used is μX_i, only the OLS estimator for β_i is biased, and the bias can be corrected by multiplying the estimate by μ.

The range of types of *nonlinear* errors (that are a function of the variable being measured) is limitless, as any error that is not an intercept or scale error (or a combination thereof) is nonlinear. For instance, if all respondents underreport their weight, but the size of the underreporting (in percentage terms) increases as true weight increases, so that heavier women tend to "lie" by a greater amount, the resulting NRME would be nonlinear. Only when the functional form of the nonlinear error is evident is it possible to correct for the bias in parameter estimators. For example, if our underreported weight scores were known to conform to the equation, $\text{WEIGHT}_j' = \text{WEIGHT}_j - \mu\text{WEIGHT}_j^2$, where WEIGHT' is the error-laden indicator of the true score WEIGHT, the bias in parameter estimators could be corrected. And, of course, the solution requiring the least effort in such a case is to adjust scores for the indicator of weight before regression analysis, so that an error-free dependent variable is used in the regression estimation.

Two particular forms of nonlinear error as a function of the variable being measured are worthy of special attention. One can be called *error toward moderation*. This kind of error can be expected when measurement is based on survey responses to questions for which respondents feel some social pressure to appear "moderate." Namboodiri et al. (1975, p. 578) speculate that when asked questions designed to measure

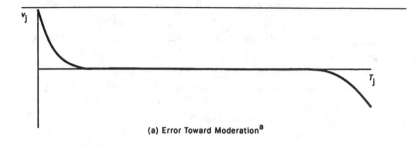

(a) Error Toward Moderation[a]

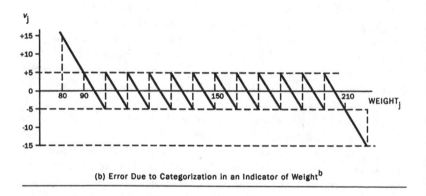

(b) Error Due to Categorization in an Indicator of Weight[b]

Figure 5.5. Two Forms of Nonlinear NRME as a Function of the Variable Being Measured

NOTES: a. This graph portrays the relationship between T_j and v_j in the measurement model, $I_j = T_j + v_j$, where I is the indicator of the true score, T. If there were no measurement error (so that $v_j = 0$ for all j), the curve depicting the relationship would be the horizontal axis itself.

b. This graph portrays the relationship between $WEIGHT_j$ and v_j in the measurement model, $WEIGHT_j' = WEIGHT_j + v_j$, where $WEIGHT'$ is an indicator of $WEIGHT$.

ideology on a liberal-conservative dimension, extremists at both ends of the scale try to appear more moderate in their views. A desire to appear moderate would result in NRME taking a form similar to that graphed in Figure 5.5(a). If T_j in the figure represents the concept "liberalism of ideology," the graph shows that the ideology indicator reflects the true scores of "moderates" without error. But the indicator is biased downward for "ultraliberals" and upward for "ultraconservatives."

Similarly, if the exercise variable in our weight illustration were measured by an indicator based on self-reports, and complete "couch potatoes" tend to report getting *some* exercise, whereas "exercise freaks" tend to try to appear more moderate in their activity, Figure 5.5(a) might also portray accurately the measurement error in the true score, EXERCISE.

Another common form of NRME as a function of the variable being measured is *error due to categorization.*[42] This occurs when a continuous variable is measured by placing objects in a set of ordered categories. When an analyst is using secondary data reported in categories, such error is unavoidable. But some doing research will categorize a continuous variable when they believe that the variable is measured with error, based on a belief that categorization will somehow *diminish* the error. But categorization is never a cure for random measurement error, and virtually never a cure for nonrandom error, as, generally, the process just adds a new form of NRME to whatever measurement error is already present. For example, assume that WEIGHT is a perfect measure of true weight, but that we (a) categorize it in 10-pound intervals, 100-110, 110-120, . . . , 190-200, and assign all women the score at the center of the interval (i.e., 105, 115, . . . , 195, respectively); and (b) score all individuals weighing less than 100 pounds 95, and all persons weighing more than 200 pounds 205. Such a categorization yields the measurement error reflected in Figure 5.5(b), where the graph of the relationship between the true score and the size of the measurement error is a series of disconnected negatively sloped segments. Persons weighing exactly 95 pounds, 105 pounds, . . . , or 205 pounds would be measured without error. But all other measures would be in error. For people weighing between 90 and 210, the magnitude of the measurement error would always be less than 5 pounds, but the weight scores for very light or very heavy persons would reflect greater error.

The distortion from measurement error due to categorization becomes more severe as the number of categories used decreases. Although the above 12-category weight scale (with mostly 10-pound intervals) would probably produce relatively little bias in coefficient estimators, dichotomizing weight scores into two categories could produce serious distortion. Indeed, in extreme cases, measurement error due to categorization can actually shift the expected value of a parameter estimator from positive to negative (or vice versa), thereby prompting a dramatically incorrect substantive conclusion. As an example, if we measure weight in our hypothetical population with a dichotomous measure of 1 ("heavy") or 0 ("light") using 150 pounds as an arbitrary

TABLE 5.3

Illustration of Effects of Measurement Error Due to Categorization:
The Implications of "Dichotomizing" the Weight Variable[a]

Independent Variable	Parameter	(1) Expected Value of Parameter Estimator With NRME[b]	(2) Population Value (Without Measurement Error)[c]
Intercept	α	−1.19	38.10
CALORIES	β_C	0.00059	0.0291
FAT	β_F	−0.032	−3.098
EXERCISE	β_E	0.0013	−0.1183
HEIGHT	β_H	0.0102	1.346
AGE	β_A	−0.0038	−0.285
SMOKER	β_S	0.167	3.01
FAT^2	β_{FF}	0.00105	0.084
SMOKER • EXERCISE	β_{SE}	−0.0024	0.1097
METABOLISM	β_M	−0.289	−1.795

NOTES: a. That is, when WEIGHT is measured as 0 = "light" (< 150 pounds) and 1 = "heavy" (> 150 pounds).
b. Obtained by running OLS regression on the full population of 134 women using the dichotomous indicator of weight.
c. As presented in the text.

boundary between categories, the expected values of the parameter estimators for Equation 3.1 are as reported in Column 1 of Table 5.3. These expected parameter estimators can be compared with the true parameters (i.e., the expected parameters when WEIGHT is measured without error), which are reproduced in Column 2. The expected parameter estimators "with error" differ in sign from the expected estimators "without error" for two independent variables—EXERCISE, and the product SMOKER • EXERCISE—and the implications for the substantive interpretation of the effects of smoking and exercise on weight are striking. As noted in Chapter 3, the true parameters imply that among *nonsmokers* an increase in energy expenditure from vigorous exercise of 100 calories/day results in an expected decrease of 11.8 pounds (when all other independent variables are held constant), whereas among *smokers* the same increase in exercise causes, on average, only a .86-pound weight reduction. But the analysis with a dichotomous (error-laden) dependent variable suggests that among *nonsmokers* an increase of 100 calories/day in vigorous exercise leads to an *increase* of .13 in the probability of being "heavy" when all other independent variables are held constant, whereas among *smokers* the same increase in exercise produces a *decrease* of .11 in the chances of being "heavy."[43]

NRME as a function of *extraneous variables* can also be formalized by Equation 5.15; in this case, v is not a function of T, but of other variables. In some situations, this form of NRME has easily predictable consequences. For example, if the error in the indicator (Y') for the dependent variable (Y) is linearly related to one of the independent variables (X_i) in the regression model, so that $Y_j' = Y_j + \mu X_{ij}$, substitution of the expression for Y' in Equation 2.2, followed by a manipulation of terms, shows that (a) the estimators for all parameters except β_i are completely unaffected by the measurement error, and (b) the biased estimator for β_i can be corrected by subtracting the constant μ from it. This form of NRME might occur in our illustration, where Y represents WEIGHT, X_i denotes EXERCISE, and $\mu < 0$, if weight were self-reported and women who exercise frequently were more "sensitive" about being "overweight" than women who get less exercise. Then the magnitude of underreporting would be directly related to amount of vigorous physical activity.

But more complicated forms of NRME as a function of extraneous variables can have consequences that are more difficult to predict. For instance, assume that self-reports uniformly underestimate true weight, but that people who are heavy relative to their height "lie" the most, so that the magnitude of measurement error is given by $v_j = [(1.2)(\text{WEIGHT}_j/\text{HEIGHT}_j)]^2$. In this case, measurement error in the dependent variable is a nonlinear function of the variable being measured and one of the independent variables. Column 1 of Table 5.4 shows the expected values of coefficient estimators for Equation 3.1 when the dependent variable is replaced by this error-laden indicator. These expected parameter estimators can be compared with the true population parameters in Column 2 to yield the measure of "relative" bias developed above and presented in Column 3. Although Table 5.4 shows that the bias due to the NRME is insufficient to change the sign of any coefficient, the parameter estimators *over*estimate the magnitude of the effect of HEIGHT, whereas the magnitude of effects of the other variables tend to be *under*estimated by from 8% to 13%.

PROXY VARIABLES

A final warning about measurement error pertains to the use of a *proxy* variable, a variable assumed to be correlated with the concept of interest that is used to measure the concept when it cannot be measured

58

TABLE 5.4
Illustration of Effects of Measurement Error as a Function of
Extraneous Variables: Measurement Error in the Weight Variable
as a Nonlinear Function of Itself and Height[a]

Independent Variable	Parameter	(1) Expected Value of Parameter Estimator With NRME	(2) Population Value (Without Measurement Error)[b]	(3) Percentage Bias as a Result of Measurement Error[c]
Intercept	α	26.56	38.10	−0.30
CALORIES	β_C	0.0262	0.0291	−0.10
FAT	β_F	−2.705	−3.098	−0.13
EXERCISE	β_E	−0.1085	−0.1183	−0.08
HEIGHT	β_H	1.426	1.346	0.06
AGE	β_A	−0.255	−0.285	−0.11
SMOKER	β_S	2.68	3.01	−0.11
FAT^2	β_{FF}	0.073	0.084	−0.13
SMOKER · EXERCISE	β_{SE}	0.0996	0.1097	−0.09
METABOLISM	β_M	−1.612	−1.795	−0.10

NOTES: a. When the true score, $WEIGHT_j$, is measured by $WEIGHT_j - [(1.2)(WEIGHT_j/HEIGHT_j)]^2$.
b. As presented in the text.
c. (Value in Column 1 − value in Column 2)/value in Column 2.

directly. For example, a state or nation's per capita income is often used as a proxy for its level of development (e.g., Dye, 1966; Pryor, 1968). In an illustration from the weight model, if data on saturated fat intake (FAT) were not available for a sample of cases, one might consider as a proxy the percentage of meals that a woman eats at fast-food restaurants. When proxy variables are utilized, analysts can be lured into a false conclusion of valid measurement if there is little error in the measurement of the proxy itself. But, for instance, knowledge that per capita income is measured without any error would not be evidence of the absence of error in the measurement of the concept of level of development when income is used as a proxy. Consequently, researchers must be alert to two possible sources of measurement error when proxy variables are used as indicators: (a) random or nonrandom error in the measurement of the true score for the *proxy* and (b) nonrandom error resulting from the inability of the true score on the proxy to reflect perfectly the concept being measured.

Economists and other social scientists frequently rely on proxy variables when they measure "demand," "support," or "interest" using spending data. Examples include measuring (a) a household's *demand* for a good by its expenditure, (b) an individual's *support* for a cause by the amount he or she contributes to associated groups, and (c) a community's *interest* in a sporting event by the number of tickets sold.[44] With such spending variables, we must be sensitive to both errors in measuring spending (or tickets sold) and errors owing to the failure of spending (or tickets sold) to reflect accurately the level of demand, support, or interest. Among individuals who make contributions, the amount contributed may measure support for the cause with very little error. But if some minimum level of (nonzero) support is necessary to motivate a contribution, the presence of individuals who contribute nothing would lead to substantial measurement error. Because a contribution is constrained to be no less than zero (i.e., since it is *censored* at zero), individuals who just barely miss surpassing the threshold level of support necessary to contribute would have the same support score as persons who are violently opposed to the cause. This would result in NRME in which the magnitude of the error is a function of the true score; for persons whose true (support) score is below the threshold, the lower the level of support, the greater the amount by which the contribution (of zero) overmeasures the true score.[45]

In some cases, a variable that is quantitative becomes nonquantitative when used as a proxy to measure another concept; this occurs when the proxy variable is monotonically—but not linearly—related to the concept being measured. The number of children in a family is unquestionably a (discrete) quantitative variable, as the difference between values on the scale accurately reflects the "distance" between cases with regard to number of children. However, when number of children is used as a proxy to measure "time spent by a parent taking care of children," it seems reasonable to assume that the difference between 0 children and 1 child represents a greater difference in time spent than the difference between 4 and 5 children. This would mean that number of children would fail to be quantitative when used as an indicator of time spent caring for children. Even variables that are continuous may lose their quantitative character when used as proxies to measure other concepts. For instance, Carter (1971) contends that income is nonlinearly related to social status, as a difference of $10,000 in annual income indicates a greater difference in status at very low levels of income than at high levels. Consequently, when income is used as a proxy for social status, the indicator is no longer quantitative. If a researcher is confident about the specific nature of the nonlinear relationship between a concept and its proxy indicator, a mathematical transformation can be used to "stretch" and "shrink" distances at appropriate ranges of the measurement scale to construct a quantitative indicator; accordingly, Carter (1971) recommends using the logarithm of income to measure status.

The Assumptions of Linearity and Additivity

Determining whether a linear additive model is appropriate in a concrete research application requires the researcher to consider whether, for each independent variable, the slope of the relationship between it and the expected value of the dependent variable depends on the context—the value of that independent variable and/or the value of other independent variables. If the theory suggests that the change in the expected value of Y resulting from a small fixed increase in the independent variable X_1 (i.e., if the theory suggests that the slope of the relationship between X_1 and the expected value of Y) depends on the value of X_1, a *nonlinear* specification is required. If the theory predicts that the change in the expected value of Y associated with a small increase in X_1 depends on the value of one or more of the other independent variables, a *nonadditive* or *interactive* specification is appropriate.

If a nonlinear and/or nonadditive specification is required, it is the specific nature of the nonlinearity and/or interaction that determines whether the analyst can stay within the confines of ordinary least squares estimation, or must abandon OLS in favor of other estimation techniques. If some mathematical transformation can be used to convert a nonlinear and/or nonadditive model into an equivalent linear additive equation, the model is termed *intrinsically linear and additive*;[46] also, the model is said to be nonlinear and/or nonadditive with respect to the *variables*, but linear and additive with respect to the *parameters*. A nonlinear and/or nonadditive model that is intrinsically linear and additive, and that, after being suitably transformed, satisfies the Gauss-Markov assumptions, can be estimated appropriately via OLS regression. In contrast, nonlinear and/or nonadditive models that are *intrinsically* so—that is, that are nonlinear and/or nonadditive with respect to the *parameters*—can never be estimated reasonably with OLS; instead, procedures such as nonlinear least squares and maximum likelihood estimation should be used (Fox, 1984, pp. 206-213; Greene, 1990, pp. 335-340; Kmenta, 1986, pp. 512-517).

We can specify a general version of a regression model that is linear and additive with respect to parameters as follows:

$$f(Y_j) = g_0(\alpha) + \beta_1 g_1(X_{1j}, X_{2j}, \ldots, X_{rj}) \qquad [5.16]$$
$$+ \beta_2 g_2(X_{1j}, X_{2j}, \ldots, X_{rj}) + \ldots + \beta_k g_k(X_{1j}, X_{2j}, \ldots, X_{rj}) + h(\varepsilon_j),$$

where, as usual, α, β_1, β_2, ..., β_k are parameters; f is a function of the variable Y; g_0 is a function of the intercept; h is a function of the error term; and each of g_1, g_2, ..., g_k is a function of a set of r independent variables. By using functions (for f, the various gs, and h) involving powers, logarithms, ratios, and products of variables—as well as others—the form of Equation 5.16 allows for a variety of types of nonlinearity and/or nonadditivity with respect to variables.

For example, the illustrative weight model of Equation 3.1 includes a term applying the "squaring" function to the variable FAT to specify a type of nonlinearity in the relationship between fat intake and weight.[47] In another example, the term (SMOKER • EXERCISE) in Equation 3.1 is a "multiplicative" function of SMOKER and EXERCISE, and the inclusion of this product term specifies that SMOKER and EXERCISE interact in influencing a woman's weight. Other commonly used nonlinear and/or nonadditive specifications that are intrinsically linear and additive include the following:

$$Y_j = \alpha + \beta(1/X_j) + \varepsilon_j \quad \text{(a hyperbolic or reciprocal model),}[48]$$

$$\log Y_j = \alpha + \beta X_j + \varepsilon_j \quad \text{(a semilog model),}$$

$$\log Y_j = \alpha + \beta \log X_j + \log \varepsilon_j \quad \text{(an exponential model), and}$$

$$\log Y_j = \log \alpha + \beta_1 \log X_{1j} + \beta_2 \log X_{2j} + \log \varepsilon_j \quad \text{(a log-log model).}[49]$$
$$[5.17]$$

The last of these models is a nonlinear nonadditive specification known as the *Cobb-Douglas function*, which is most commonly expressed in its equivalent pretransformation form:[50]

$$Y_j = \alpha X_{1j}^{\beta_1} X_{2j}^{\beta_2} \varepsilon_j . \qquad [5.18]$$

This equation can be transformed into Equation 5.17 by taking logs of both sides of the equation. But note that our ability to "linearize" Equation 5.18 in this fashion hinges on the model having an error term with a *multiplicative* effect on Y. In contrast, a model similar to Equation 5.18, but having a conventional additive disturbance term,

$$Y_j = \alpha X_{1j}^{\beta_1} X_{2j}^{\beta_2} + \varepsilon_j$$

is nonlinear and nonadditive with respect to the parameters, because it cannot be converted to an equivalent linear additive equation through any transformation.

If one's theory points to nonlinear and/or interactive effects, yet an estimation model that is linear and additive with respect to variables (i.e., that includes no "transformed" functions of variables) is used, a form of specification error occurs. In some situations, the misspecification of functional form can be interpreted equivalently as a specification error resulting from the exclusion of relevant variables. For example, assume that the frame of reference is the weight model of Equation 3.1, and that the estimation model includes all the independent variables in the reference model, but in a *linear additive* equation, ignoring (a) the interaction between smoking and exercise in their effect on weight and (b) the nonlinear relationship between fat intake and weight:

$$
\begin{aligned}
WEIGHT_j = {} & \alpha + \beta_C CALORIES_j + \beta_F FAT_j + \beta_E EXERCISE_j \\
& + \beta_H HEIGHT_j + \beta_A AGE_j + \beta_S SMOKER_j \\
& + \beta_M METABOLISM_j + u_{Wj} . \quad \text{[estimation model]} \quad [5.19]
\end{aligned}
$$

In the case of partial slope coefficients for reference-model independent variables that are linearly and additively related to the dependent variable (i.e., CALORIES, HEIGHT, AGE, and METABOLISM), one can assess the distortion caused by the incorrect specification of functional form by analyzing the bias resulting from the exclusion of the regressors FAT^2 and (SMOKER • EXERCISE) from the regression. Given our knowledge of the consequences of specification errors of exclusion, we can conclude that the parameter estimator for any independent variable correlated with FAT^2 or SMOKER • EXERCISE will be biased.

But in the case of the independent variable, FAT, that is nonlinearly related to the dependent variable, or in the case of those variables—

EXERCISE and SMOKER—that interact in influencing the dependent variable, the distortion in the OLS estimators for Equation 5.19 goes well beyond "bias" in the traditional sense of the word. This is because in the estimation model, the parameter being estimated—regardless of its expected value—has an interpretation fundamentally inconsistent with the assumptions of the reference model. Linear additive Equation 5.19 assumes that the effects of all independent variables on WEIGHT are *constant*; they do not vary with the values of the independent variables. Consequently, if the parameters for Regression Model 3.1 were mistakenly estimated using Equation 5.19, *any* estimates of the assumed-to-be-*constant* slopes would fundamentally misrepresent the *varying* strengths of the effects of FAT, SMOKER, and EXERCISE across different values of these independent variables.

In certain very specific situations, the effects of incorrectly specifying a nonlinear and/or nonadditive model as linear and additive with respect to variables are readily predictable. For example, assume that the reference model is a second-order polynomial equation,

$$Y_j = \alpha_j + \beta_1 X_j + \beta_2 X_j^2 + \varepsilon_j, \quad \text{[frame of reference]} \quad [5.20]$$

where the independent variable, X, is measured by its deviation from the mean.[51] Suppose that a researcher mistakenly specifies the relationship between X and Y as linear:

$$Y_j = \alpha_j + \beta_1 X_j + u_j \quad (\text{where } u_j = \varepsilon_j + \beta_2 X_j^2). \quad \text{[estimation model] } [5.21]$$

It can then be shown that the expected value of the OLS estimator for β_1 is given by the formula (Theil, 1971, p. 550)[52]

$$E(b_1) = \beta_1 + \beta_2 [E(X^3)/E(X^2)].$$

Thus the bias as a result of specification error is $\beta_2[E(X^3)/E(X^2)]$. The sign of $E(X^3)/E(X^2)$ is determined by the *skewness* of the distribution for the independent variable.[53] When the distribution for X is *symmetric*, $E(X^3)$ equals 0,[54] and thus the bias is zero. If the distribution is *skewed*, the sign of the bias is determined by the signs of $E(X^3)$ and β_2, because $E(X^2)$ is always positive. When the distribution for X is positively skewed (with more extremely large values of X than small, so that the mean of X is greater than the median), $E(X^3) > 0$, but when the distribution is negatively skewed (so that the median is greater than the mean), $E(X^3) < 0$. Therefore, we can conclude that when X is measured as a deviation from the mean, and the distribution for X is symmetric, OLS estimation of the incorrectly specified linear model of Equation 5.21 still yields an unbiased estimate of β_1. In a similar fashion that Formula 3.2 was determined, it can be shown that at any given value, X^*, of the independent variable, X, the slope of the relationship between X_j and $E(Y|X_j)$ in Equation 5.20 is equal to $\beta_1 + (2\beta_2 X^*)$. Thus when $X = 0$, the slope of this relationship is β_1. This means that when X is measured by the deviation from its mean, and is symmetric, estimation of the incorrectly specified linear model will, on average, yield a slope coefficient estimate equal to the slope of the polynomial curve (Equation 5.20) at the mean value of X. This is intuitively pleasing. For example, consider a polynomial model in which the slope of the relationship between X and the expected value of Y varies between a low of c and a high of d as X varies across its full range of possible values. It makes sense that when such a model is mistakenly specified as linear, the linear model will tend to produce an estimate of the constant slope that is greater than c but less than d.

This property characterizes the multivariate weight model of Equation 3.1 as well. For this model, the slope of the relationship between FAT and expected WEIGHT varies between .26 and 5.30 as FAT increases from its low in the population of 20 grams to its high of 50 (see Figure 3.1).[55] Table 5.5 shows the effect of incorrectly specifying Equation 3.1 by assuming linearity, and thus excluding the term for FAT^2. Column 2 confirms that the expected value of the estimator for β_F in the linear model is between .26 and 5.30—taking on a value, 1.381, that diverges radically from the actual population value of -3.098. As Table 5.1 shows, the correlation between FAT and FAT^2 is extremely high at .98; thus it is no surprise that deleting FAT^2 from the model results in heavy bias in the estimator for β_F. But I have not presented a measure of bias in the estimator of β_F in Table 5.5, because the bias—the disparity between 1.381 and -3.098—is virtually meaningless as a measure of the distortion produced by the incorrect model specification. In the misspecified linear model, β_F reflects a strength of the effect of fat consumption on weight that is assumed to be *stable* across varying levels of consumption. In the nonlinear model, the strength of the effect of fat consumption on weight is assumed to *vary* depending on the level of consumption; β_F represents the strength of that effect *when fat consumption is at zero* (a level of consumption that, in fact, happens to be out of

TABLE 5.5

Illustration of Effects of Incorrect Specification of Functional Form: Treating the Nonlinear/Nonadditive Model of Equation 3.1 as Linear and as Additive

Variable	Parameter	(1) Population Value[a]	(2) Incorrect Specification as a Linear Model	(3)	(4) Incorrect Specification as an Additive Model	(5)
			Expected Value of Parameter Estimator When FAT^2 Is Excluded	Percentage Bias as a Result of Incorrect Specification[b]	Expected Value of Parameter Estimator When (SMOKER · EXERCISE) Is Excluded	Percentage Bias as a Result of Incorrect Specification[c]
Intercept	α	38.10	−33.98	−1.89	28.06	−0.26
CALORIES	β_C	0.0291	0.0307	0.05	0.0295	0.01
FAT	β_F	−3.098	1.381	**	−2.984	−0.04
EXERCISE	β_E	−0.1183	−0.0748	−0.37	−0.0939	**
HEIGHT	β_H	1.346	1.426	0.06	1.447	0.08
AGE	β_A	−0.285	−0.136	−0.52	−0.267	−0.06
SMOKER	β_S	3.01	5.08	0.69	4.91	**
FAT^2	β_{FF}	0.084	—	—	0.082	−0.02
SMOKER · EXERCISE	β_{SE}	0.1097	0.0739	−0.33	—	—
METABOLISM	β_M	−1.795	−1.750	−0.03	−1.809	0.01

NOTES: a. As presented in the text.
b. (Value in Column 2 − value in Column 1)/value in Column 1.
c. (Value in Column 4 − value in Column 1)/value in Column 1.
**Measure of bias not meaningful for this estimator.

the range of values reflected in the population);[56] at other levels of consumption, the strength of the effect is a function of both β_F and β_{FF}.

Columns 2 and 3 of Table 5.5 confirm that specifying the relationship between fat intake and weight as linear also results in bias in the parameters for other predictors of weight. For example, the effect of smoking on weight among women who get no vigorous exercise (as reflected by β_S) tends to be overestimated by 69% when FAT^2 is excluded from the model. Also, the expected parameter estimator for β_A (reflecting the impact of age) underestimates the actual magnitude of the effect by 52%.

Table 5.5 also presents an analysis of the effects of mistakenly specifying the "weight" reference model as *additive*, by excluding the multiplicative term, SMOKER • EXERCISE (see Columns 4 and 5). As one might anticipate, the expected value of β_E in the incorrectly specified additive model (−0.0939)—which represents the constant slope of the relationship between EXERCISE and the expected value of WEIGHT— lies between the true slope among nonsmokers (β_E = −0.1183) and the true slope among smokers ($\beta_E + \beta_{SE}$ = −0.0086). But an estimator of the *constant* effect of either vigorous exercise or smoking on a woman's weight in an additive model inherently fails to reflect accurately a true relationship in which the effect of smoking on weight varies depending on the amount of exercise a woman gets, and the effect of exercise is different among smokers than among nonsmokers.

An examination of the correlation matrix in Table 5.1 might lead us to anticipate that excluding SMOKER • EXERCISE would lead to less bias in partial slope coefficient estimators for other variables than excluding FAT^2, as SMOKER • EXERCISE is weakly correlated with all variables except SMOKER and EXERCISE. And indeed, for all partial slope coefficients (except β_S and β_E), the expected value of the estimator in the incorrectly specified model is always less than 8% over or under the population parameter (see Column 5 of Table 5.5). But there is no general reason to expect that incorrectly specifying an interactive model as additive should produce less bias than mistakenly specifying a nonlinear model as linear.

In many cases, it seems that linear and additive models are chosen for analysis because social scientists fail to think about whether nonlinear or nonadditive relationships might be theoretically anticipated. But it is not enough to "brainstorm" about the variables that might affect a dependent variable, and then merely insert indicators for these variables as regressors in a standard linear, additive regression model. A reliance on a model that is linear and additive with respect to variables implies an assumption of enormous substantive import: that the effect of each independent variable on the dependent variable is completely independent of the values at which the independent variables are fixed. Consequently, the brainstorming prior to model specification must include an analysis of how the effect of each independent variable on the dependent variable can be expected to vary as that—and other—independent variables change in value.[57] Only when the expected natures of these changing effects are clarified substantively can an analyst meaningfully choose an appropriate functional form for the regression model.

The Assumptions of Homoscedasticity and Lack of Autocorrelation

The *homoscedasticity* assumption (A6) is that the conditional variance of the error term in a regression model is constant, that is, that in Equation 2.2, $VAR(\varepsilon_j|X_{1j}, X_{2j}, \ldots, X_{kj}) = \sigma^2$, where σ^2 is a constant. *Heteroscedasticity* occurs when the conditional variance of the error term is *not* constant. Then, symbolically, we can write $VAR(\varepsilon_j|X_{1j}, X_{2j}, \ldots, X_{kj}) = \sigma_j^2$. The assumption that the error terms for any two observations are uncorrelated (A7) is called the absence of *autocorrelation* or *serial correlation*. We will examine the substantive meanings of the assumptions of heteroscedasticity and lack of autocorrelation separately, but briefly consider the implications of violating these assumptions together, because the basic consequences of violating the two assumptions are identical. As we shall see, in the presence of heteroscedasticity or autocorrelation, OLS coefficient estimators are unbiased but not BLUE; an alternative technique called *generalized least squares* (GLS) produces estimators that are BLUE.

THE SUBSTANTIVE MEANING OF AUTOCORRELATION

As with all assumptions about the error term in a regression equation, understanding the substantive meaning of a lack of autocorrelation hinges on a recognition that the error term represents the combined impact of those variables affecting the dependent variable but not included as regressors in the model, plus any random component in the behavior of the dependent variable. If we denote these neglected variables by $Z_1, \ldots, Z_m$ (as in Equation 5.3), we can see that the assumption of a lack of autocorrelation requires that for any pair of observations (j and h), the net impacts of the excluded variables and the random component on the value of Y—$\delta_0 + (\sum_{i=1}^{m} \delta_i Z_{ij}) + R_j$, and $\delta_0 + (\sum_{i=1}^{m} \delta_i Z_{ih}) + R_h$—are uncorrelated.

Autocorrelation is especially likely to be a problem in *time-series* regression models. To see why this is so, consider a time-series model in which each of the excluded variables ($Z_1, \ldots, Z_m$) composing the error term is positively autocorrelated, that is, such that current values of the variable are positively correlated with previous values.[58] Variables that change "incrementally" over time will tend to be autocorrelated. In particular, the many social, political, and economic variables that tend to increase gradually over time (e.g., the population of California, the income of an individual, or expenditures for some organization or government) will be autocorrelated. Attitudes that tend to be reasonably stable will also be autocorrelated.

Now, consider the error terms for two successive observations (at times t and $t + 1$):

$$\varepsilon_t = \delta_0 + \delta_1 Z_{1t} + \delta_2 Z_{2t} + \ldots + \delta_m Z_{mt} + R_t \qquad [5.22]$$

and

$$\varepsilon_{t+1} = \delta_0 + \delta_1 Z_{1,t+1} + \delta_2 Z_{2,t+1} + \ldots + \delta_m Z_{m,t+1} + R_{t+1}. \qquad [5.23]$$

(For time-series equations, we will use t instead of j to denote the observation, as a reminder that the variation in the model is over *time*.) To make the mathematics easier, we assume that all the Zs have been adjusted to have a zero mean. Taking the mean of both sides of Equation 5.22 yields[59]

$$E(\varepsilon_t) = E(\delta_0) + \delta_1 E(Z_{1t}) + \delta_2 E(Z_{2t}) + \ldots + \delta_m E(Z_{mt}) + E(R_t). \qquad [5.24]$$

$E(\varepsilon_t) = 0$ (as presumed in A4); by assumption, $E(Z_{1t}) = E(Z_{2t}) = \ldots = E(Z_{mt}) = 0$; and $E(R_t) = 0$, because R represents inherent randomness in the behavior of Y. Substituting zeros for all these means in Equation 5.24 implies that $E(\delta_0)$ also equals zero, and hence that the constant δ_0 must be zero. Consequently, Equations 5.22 and 5.23 reduce to

$$\varepsilon_t = R_t + \sum_{i=1}^{m} \delta_i Z_{it} \quad \text{and} \quad \varepsilon_{t+1} = R_{t+1} + \sum_{i=1}^{m} \delta_i Z_{i,t+1} \,.$$

Then we can make use of the definition of the covariance to write[60]

$$COV(\varepsilon_t, \varepsilon_{t+1}) = E(\varepsilon_t \varepsilon_{t+1}) = E[(R_t + \sum_{i=1}^{m} \delta_i Z_{it})(R_{t+1} + \sum_{i=1}^{m} \delta_i Z_{i,t+1})] \,. \qquad [5.25]$$

The last expression in Equation 5.25 can be manipulated to yield the following expression for the covariance between successive error terms:

$$COV(\varepsilon_t, \varepsilon_{t+1}) = E(R_t \sum_{i=1}^{m} \delta_i Z_{i,t+1}) + E(R_{t+1} \sum_{i=1}^{m} \delta_i Z_{it}) \qquad [5.26]$$

$$+ E(R_t R_{t+1}) + \sum_{i=1}^{m} \sum_{j=1}^{m} \delta_i \delta_j E(Z_{it} Z_{j,t+1}) \,.$$

The fact that R_t and R_{t+1} have mean zero implies that each of the first three terms on the right side of Equation 5.26 is a covariance between a random variable (R_t or R_{t+1}) and some other variable, and therefore must be zero (see note 60). Thus these three terms "drop out" of the sum on the right side of Equation 5.26, leaving

$$\text{COV}(\varepsilon_t, \varepsilon_{t+1}) = \sum_{i=1}^{m} \sum_{j=1}^{m} \delta_i \delta_j E(Z_{it} Z_{j,t+1}) . \qquad [5.27]$$

Is it reasonable to assume that this covariance is zero as the regression assumption requires?

We consider first the sum of the subset of terms in Equation 5.27 for which $i = j$:

$$\sum_{i=1}^{m} \delta_i^2 E(Z_{it} Z_{i,t+1}) . \qquad [5.28]$$

This expression is a weighted sum over all excluded Zs of the covariance between the values of the variable at successive points in time. First, note that all the weights (δ_i^2) in the sum—being squares of coefficients—are positive. Moreover, we have assumed that each of the Zs is positively autocorrelated, which implies that each of the covariances [$E(Z_{it} Z_{i,t+1})$] in the sum is positive. So all the terms in the weighted sum are positive, and thus the sum itself is positive.

One cannot generalize so easily about the signs of the terms for which $i \neq j$ in the summation of Equation 5.27. But, at least in a situation in which *both the dependent variable and the bulk of the independent variables tend to increase gradually over time*, one can expect that most of the $E(Z_{it} Z_{j,t+1})$ terms in the sum should be positive, as most Z variables at time t should be positively correlated with most other Z variables at time $t + 1$. Also, in such a situation, the bulk of the δ coefficients—which measure the effects of the excluded Zs on the dependent variable—should be positive. If this is the case, most of the terms for which $i \neq j$ in the summation of Equation 5.27 should be positive. Therefore, when these terms are added to the sum in 5.28 (for which $i = j$), the ultimate value of the covariance between successive observations of the error term should be positive. This suggests why autocorrelation can be expected to be a common problem in time-series regression models.

As an illustration of the substantive meaning of autocorrelation, we can consider the weight example in a time-series context, where we assume we have a regression model predicting an individual's weight at the beginning of each week.[61] In this time-series application, one of the important variables subsumed in the error term might be the individual's health. Assuming an individual's health is uncorrelated with the independent variables in the model,[62] leaving health out of the model would not result in biased estimators. But the health of an individual is likely autocorrelated, as the state of one's health this week should be a fairly good predictor of the state of one's health next week, and this characteristic of a person's health would contribute toward positive autocorrelation in the regression model's disturbance term.

Sometimes, the excluded variables that produce autocorrelation can be conceived as events that take place and, in effect, create a "shock" in the system that carries forward into future time periods. For instance, consider a time-series model attempting to explain the average price of a home in San Francisco. The 1989 earthquake might have resulted in a shock to the pricing system that has an impact over a period of time. If so, and this event is not explicitly specified in the model, autocorrelation will be present. In effect, the implicit variable missing from the equation will be "fear of earthquakes," a variable that took on a high value in 1989 and will probably tend to be high for several years thereafter.

Given that autocorrelation in the "excluded" variables constituting an error term can produce a disturbance term that is autocorrelated, it should not be surprising that specification errors of exclusion in time-series models also can lead to autocorrelation. To see why this is true, assume that a frame of reference model with error term ε is estimated with a regression model omitting the independent variable, X_1. If X_1 is autocorrelated, then the disturbance term for the estimation model, $u_t = \varepsilon_t + \beta_1 X_{1t}$, is also likely autocorrelated. However, in the case of a specification error of exclusion, where the omitted variable cannot generally be assumed to be uncorrelated with the independent variables, the autocorrelation is usually a secondary problem, because the bias in coefficient estimators resulting from the specification error is typically more serious than the consequences of the autocorrelation.

Another form of specification error that can result in autocorrelation in time-series models is an incorrect functional form. For instance, assume that the frame of reference model is the nonlinear polynomial equation

$$Y_t = \alpha + \beta_1 X_t + \beta_2 X_t^2 + \varepsilon_t \quad \text{[frame of reference]}$$

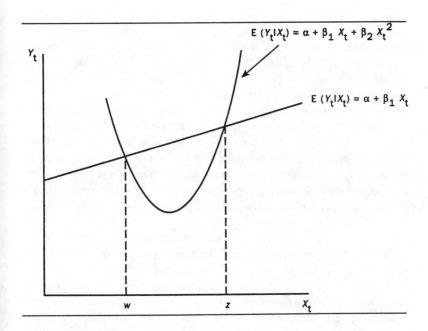

Figure 5.6. Illustration of Autocorrelation Associated With an Incorrect Functional Form in a Time-Series Model

graphed in Figure 5.6, but that a linear model

$$Y_t = \alpha + \beta_1 X_t + u_t \quad \text{[estimation model]}$$

(where $u_t = \varepsilon_t + \beta_2 X_t^2$) is instead estimated. As the graph makes clear, the incorrect functional form yields an error term, u, which tends to be positive at low or high values of the independent variable (i.e., if $X_t <$ w or $X_t > z$, $E(u_t|X_t) > 0$), and negative at "central" values of X (i.e., if $w < X_t < z$, $E(u_t|X_t) < 0$). *If X is a variable that tends to increase in value over time*, the error terms for successive observations will be correlated.

Although autocorrelation is typically not as great a concern in cross-sectional models as in time-series designs, *spatial autocorrelation* is possible in some situations. Indeed, autocorrelation should be suspected whenever the positions of the observations under analysis are "structured" relative to one another in some manner. This is clearly the case in time-series models, where observations are structured in a time sequence. When the observations under analysis are isolated persons who have little or no contact with one another—as in a random sample from a nation's population used for survey research—such a structure is almost certainly absent, and autocorrelation is unlikely to be a problem. But consider the situation if the population of women in our weight illustration were to live in one of four dormitories, each of which is structured communally so that residents spend much of their time with each other. And suppose, once again, that a woman's health is one of the variables that affects her weight, but that health is left out of the regression model. In a communal living environment, health is likely to be *spatially correlated*; as communicable diseases spread through the environment, a woman's state of health should tend to be correlated with the health of her building-mates. Autocorrelation would be the result.

Another substantive context in which analysts need to be concerned with the possibility of spatial autocorrelation is when the units observed are political jurisdictions, such as cities in a metropolitan area, states in the United States, or countries on a continent (Odland, 1988). In such situations, the variables excluded from regression analyses explaining social, political, or economic characteristics of the jurisdictions are often ones that are spatially correlated, as neighboring jurisdictions tend to be alike in a variety of respects. As a final example, consider a situation in which regression analysis is used to test a theory of the determinants of the attitudes of gay priests.[63] Because it would be difficult to enumerate the individuals in this population, constructing a random sample for empirical analysis would not be feasible. Instead, a *snowball* method might be used. In a snowball sample, only a few individuals are initially selected for interviews, but each of these individuals is asked to identify other people from the population (Sudman, 1976, pp. 210-211). Given that individuals are likely to recommend friends and acquaintances, the observations in the sample will be "structured" such that for some pairs of observations, the value for one observation of some variable that is subsumed in the regression's error term is likely to be correlated with the value for the other observation.

THE SUBSTANTIVE MEANING OF HOMOSCEDASTICITY

One important insight into the meaning of homoscedasticity is that, although it is usually stated as an assumption about the variance of the error term, it can also be cast as an assumption about the variance of the dependent variable. The error term in Equation 2.2 is termed homo-scedastic if, across each set of values for the k independent variables—

$X_{1j}, X_{2j}, \ldots, X_{kj}$—VAR$(\varepsilon_j | X_{1j}, X_{2j}, \ldots, X_{kj})$ is constant (at a value σ^2). However, for any single set of values for the Xs, $\alpha + \beta_1 X_{1j} + \beta_2 X_{2j} + \ldots + \beta_k X_{kj}$ is a constant, $E(Y_j | X_{1j}, X_{2j}, \ldots, X_{kj})$, which we will denote s_j. For this fixed set of values for the Xs, Equation 2.2 implies that $Y_j = s_j + \varepsilon_j$. Consequently, for any fixed set of independent variable values, Y and ε differ by a constant. Finally, because Y and ε differ by a constant, the conditional variances of Y and ε must be identical. This establishes that we are free to view homoscedasticity as the assumption that for each set of values of the independent variables, the conditional variance of Y equals the constant, σ^2. In understanding the substantive meaning of homoscedasticity, it can be useful to think in terms of the variance of both the error term and the dependent variable.

Whereas autocorrelation is typically associated with time-series models, heteroscedasticity is generally thought to be a problem primarily in cross-sectional research. In some cases, heteroscedasticity can result from measurement error in the dependent variable. In particular, if the amount of measurement error varies systematically across observations in cross-sectional research, then heteroscedasticity may result. For example, assume that in our continuing illustration, weight is measured through self-reports by the women under study, and that all women try to be honest, so that any measurement error is a consequence of misperception rather than misrepresentation. Suppose also that as people get older they become more "weight conscious," and thus weigh themselves more frequently. If this is the case, older women would likely provide more accurate estimates of their weight than would younger women. Thus, even if the *true variance* in weight is constant across different sets of values for the independent variables, *error variance* would decrease as age increases, leading to a negative relationship between age and the variance of the indicator for the dependent variable.

Another context in which heteroscedasticity as a consequence of measurement error can be anticipated is cross-national research. Often in such studies, the nations being analyzed vary significantly in level of development. If the dependent variable is measured with data drawn from government records, it is likely that the quality of these records will increase (and thus the degree of measurement error in the dependent variable will decrease) as level of development increases. Therefore, if any of the independent variables in the regression equation are correlated with level of development (a not unlikely situation), these variables would also tend to be correlated with the variance of the dependent variable, thereby producing heteroscedasticity.

These examples suggest that the key question the analyst must consider when assessing whether heteroscedasticity should be expected in a particular regression application is whether it is likely that the conditional variance of the error term (or, equivalently, the variance of the dependent variable) can be expected to be correlated with one or more of the independent variables in the model. If so, heteroscedasticity should be anticipated. Moreover, predictions about the specific variable(s) that are expected to be correlated with the variance of the error term are critical to determining the model respecification or estimation procedure necessary for dealing with the heteroscedasticity.

If heteroscedasticity is simply a consequence of variation in the amount of random measurement error in the dependent variable, tools are available to detect and overcome the problem. Detection relies on either visual or formal inspection of the relationship between the variance of OLS residuals and one or more of the independent variables (Kennedy, 1985, pp. 97-98).[64] Either way, the inspection requires the analyst to develop hypotheses about which independent variable(s) are related to the variance of the error term. When the heteroscedasticity suspected involves a relationship between a single independent variable and the variance of ε, a visual inspection of a graph in which regression residuals for the estimation sample are plotted against the suspected variable is often sufficient to verify heteroscedasticity (Berry & Feldman, 1985, pp. 78-80; Gujarati, 1988, pp. 327-329; Rao & Miller, 1971, pp. 116-121). But other more formal detection techniques are available, including the Goldfield-Quandt test and the Glejser test (Berry & Feldman, 1985, pp. 79-81; Gujarati, 1988, pp. 329-336; Johnson et al., 1987, pp. 303-304), approaches applicable with a single suspect independent variable, and the more general Breusch-Pagan test (Johnson et al., 1987, pp. 304-305; Kmenta, 1986, pp. 294-295), applicable when the variance of the error term is expected to be related to a linear combination of two or more variables. Once suspected heteroscedasticity is confirmed in a sample, if the analyst knows enough about its form (i.e., which independent variables are related to the variance of ε and with what functional form), generalized least squares (a technique described briefly below) can be used to yield estimators that are BLUE, thereby overcoming the heteroscedasticity problem.

But when heteroscedasticity is not a mere consequence of variation in the quality of measurement across observations, it is best to avoid considering GLS as the ideal solution. Instead, heteroscedasticity should be viewed as a signal that model respecification may be in order. In particular, heteroscedasticity may result from interaction between "included" and "excluded" independent variables. If so, the solution to heteroscedasticity would be to respecify one or more variables currently subsumed in the error term as "included" variables interacting with one or more of the "already included" independent variables.

As an illustration, we will examine a bivariate regression model in which the unit of analysis is the American family, the dependent variable is annual expenditures for vacations (to be denoted VACATION), and the independent variable is annual income (to be denoted INCOME):

$$\text{VACATION}_j = \alpha + \beta \text{INCOME}_j + \varepsilon_j. \qquad [5.29]$$

We will assume—quite noncontroversially—that the slope coefficient, β, is positive, implying that as family income increases, so does the expected amount of vacation expenditures. But not only should the mean level of vacation expenditures increase with income, the *variance* in expenditures (given a fixed level of income) should increase as income rises. Put differently, this regression model should be heteroscedastic. The logic underlying this claim is that for families with low income, the mean expenditure for vacations will be low and the variation in such expenditures will also be low, since families with low income must devote nearly all their income to necessities, leaving few funds available for travel and entertainment. But as family income rises, the amount of discretionary income increases, so that both the mean level of vacation expenditures *and* the variation of such expenditures across families will increase. Put differently, our hypothesis about the relationship between income and vacation spending is that high income is a *necessary but not sufficient* condition for large vacation expenditures.

Indeed, any time a high value for an independent variable seems to be a necessary but not sufficient condition for an observation having a high value on a dependent variable, heteroscedasticity should be suspected. Such "necessary but not sufficient" relationships yield a scatterplot for observations with a *triangular* shape. Figure 5.7(a) shows the scatterplot for a relationship between two variables, X and Y, in which a high value for X is a necessary but not sufficient condition for a high value for Y. This heteroscedasticity might be due to interaction between X and some "excluded" variable Z in influencing Y. One possibility is sketched in Figure 5.7(b), where the excluded variable Z is one that can take on three values—0, 1, and 2. The graph in Figure 5.7(b) shows the same set of observations as Figure 5.7(a), but this time interpreted in the

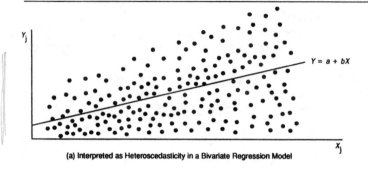

(a) Interpreted as Heteroscedasticity in a Bivariate Regression Model

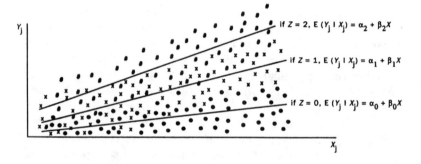

(b) Interpreted as Specification Error Resulting From Omitting the Variable Z.
NOTE: # denotes observations for which $Z = 2$, x denotes observations for which $Z = 1$,
and • denotes observations for which $Z = 0$.

Figure 5.7. Scatterplot for a "Necessary But Not Sufficient" Relationship

context of a model in which at any fixed value of Z, the relationship between X and $E(Y_j|X_j)$ is linear and the error term is homoscedastic, but the slope of the relationship between X and the expected value of Y varies with the level of Z. If the model reflected in Figure 5.7(b) were incorrectly specified with a bivariate regression of Y on X, empirical estimation would yield the pattern of heteroscedastic residuals reflected in Figure 5.7(a).

Returning to our model of vacation spending, it is important to note that the heteroscedasticity present is not a mere function of measurement error. Even if vacation expenditures were measured perfectly for all families, heteroscedasticity would still be predicted. The key questions that we, as analysts, face are (a) What excluded variables constitute the error term of Equation 5.29? and (b) Do one or more of these variables interact with family income in influencing vacation spending? The variable "the amount of satisfaction a family derives from vacations" is a likely culprit. It is reasonable to assume that a family's expenditure for vacations is determined by both the family's income and the satisfaction it derives from vacationing. And income and satisfaction from vacations can be expected to interact in influencing vacation spending. Among families that derive little satisfaction from vacations, income should have little relationship to vacation expenditures, as such families should spend only a small amount on vacations regardless of their financial resources. But as satisfaction derived from vacationing increases, the effect of income on vacation spending should grow: Among families that find vacations satisfying, those with large incomes should spend a substantial amount on vacations, but those with small incomes should be able to afford only a small amount. Thus the best solution to the heteroscedasticity problem in our vacation spending model would not be GLS estimation, but respecification as an interactive model that is arguably homoscedastic,

$$VACATION_j = \alpha + \beta_I INCOME_j + \beta_S SATISFY_j$$
$$+ \beta_{IS}[(INCOME_j)(SATISFY_j)] + \varepsilon_j \, ,$$

where SATISFY denotes the amount of satisfaction derived from vacationing. Such a model respecification avoids a "technical" solution for heteroscedasticity in favor of an enhancement of the substantive explanation of vacation spending implicit in the model.[65] Then, if the new model's error term is homoscedastic, OLS would be an appropriate estimation technique.

For a final example, we return to the weight model. Assume that we had misspecified this model, leaving out amount of exercise, and thereby resulting in the additive model

$$WEIGHT_j = \alpha + \beta_C CALORIES_j + \beta_F FAT_j + \beta_H HEIGHT_j \quad [5.30]$$
$$+ \beta_A AGE_j + \beta_S SMOKER_j + \beta_M METABOLISM_j$$
$$+ \beta_{FF} FAT_j^2 + u_j \, .$$

Given that in the population, SMOKER actually interacts with EXERCISE such that the impact of vigorous exercise on weight is greater among nonsmokers than among smokers, Equation 5.30 should be characterized by heteroscedasticity such that the variance of the error term for nonsmokers is greater than that for smokers. Given that among nonsmokers, amount of vigorous exercise has a strong effect on weight, deleting EXERCISE from the model will lead to substantial errors in the predicted weight for individuals who get an extremely large or small amount of exercise, and thus an error term with large variance. But given that among smokers, amount of exercise has a weak effect on weight, excluding EXERCISE from the model should not lead to large errors in the predicted weight for any of these individuals, and thus the error term should have a small variance.

This anticipated form of heteroscedasticity can be confirmed by running OLS regression on Equation 5.30 using the data from our population of women, and comparing the distribution of the residuals among smokers to that among nonsmokers. Figure 5.8 presents histograms for these two distributions—in Figure 5.8(a) for 40 smokers randomly selected from the population and in Figure 5.8(b) for the full population of 40 nonsmokers. (So as to keep the two histograms visually "comparable," it was important to keep sample sizes for the two distributions the same.) Even a visual inspection confirms that the distribution of residuals is more "spread out" for nonsmokers than for smokers, consistent with our analysis about the form of heteroscedasticity expected.

THE CONSEQUENCES OF
HETEROSCEDASTICITY AND AUTOCORRELATION

As noted earlier, even in the presence of heteroscedasticity or autocorrelation, OLS coefficient estimators remain unbiased. This conclusion is intuitively plausible. Consider, as an example, a *heteroscedastic* bivariate regression model

$$Y_j = \alpha + \beta X_j + \varepsilon_j$$

in which $\beta > 0$, and the variance of the error term ε increases as the value of the independent variable, X, increases, but the remainder of the standard regression assumptions hold. This means that for large values of X, there is a higher probability that observed Y values will be far away from the true regression line than for small values of X. In any one sample, a few observations at large values of X for which ε takes on an unusually large *positive* value would make the OLS estimate of the slope coefficient *greater* than β. Similarly, in any sample, a few obser-

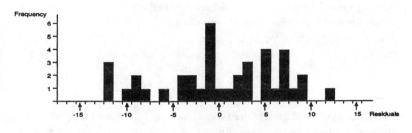

(a) Among 40 Smokers Randomly Selected from Population

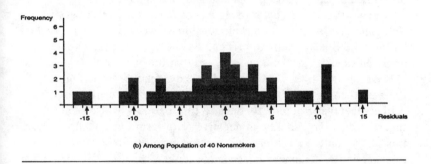

(b) Among Population of 40 Nonsmokers

Figure 5.8. Distribution of OLS Residuals for Equation 5.30

vations at large values of X for which ε takes on an unusually large *negative* value would make the OLS slope estimate *less* than β. But because the mean value of the error term is zero (assumption A4), large positive values and large negative values for ε are equally likely, so that the average slope estimate over an infinite number of random samples is still equal to β.

As an illustration of the effects of autocorrelation, consider a bivariate time-series equation,

$$Y_t = \alpha + \beta X_t + \varepsilon_t, \qquad [5.31]$$

where the cases are observations of a single individual at multiple points in time. We assume that all regression assumptions except lack of autocorrelation hold, and that the autocorrelation present takes a form commonly assumed in social science research: *positive first-order autoregressive*. In this form of autocorrelation, the value of the error term at any point in time, t, can be expressed as a function of its value at the previous time, $t - 1$, and a random variable, u:[66]

$$\varepsilon_t = \pi \varepsilon_{t-1} + u_t,$$

where π is a constant greater than 0 but less than 1.[67] In effect, the expected value of the error in one period is a fixed proportion of the error in the previous period. Moreover, the process by which the error term changes in value over time consists of two components—a systematic component (expressed by the parameter π) and a random component, u.

Suppose that X in Equation 5.31 is a variable that tends to grow over time, and that the population relationship between X and Y is graphed by the solid line in Figure 5.9. Then, assume that a sample of data were obtained to estimate the equation, and that the error term for the first observation (at time t') happened to be negative as in Figure 5.9. Because there is a positive first-order autoregressive error structure, it is likely that the error term for the next time period will also be negative. Indeed, when there is a large negative error term for any observation, it is likely that the error term will remain negative for several observations. A similar statement can be made about a large positive error term (like the one at time t'' in Figure 5.9);[68] it tends to be followed by other positive error terms. So the pattern of error reflected in Figure 5.9 would not be unusual in a given sample. An OLS estimator for β based on the sample in Figure 5.9 would clearly overestimate the slope. But over repeated samples, this error in estimation would average out to zero, because the mean value of the error term is still assumed to be zero, and therefore the first-order autoregressive error structure is in the long run equally likely to yield positive and negative values for ε. Consequently, the OLS estimator for β remains unbiased.

But with heteroscedasticity or autocorrelation, OLS estimators are no longer BLUE; instead, the estimation technique of generalized least squares yields BLUE estimators (see Hanushek & Jackson, 1977, chap. 6; Wonnacott & Wonnacott, 1979, chap. 16). The more efficient GLS estimators are determined by minimizing a *weighted* sum of squared residuals (instead of an *un*weighted sum as in the case of OLS); observations that are expected to have the largest values for the error term (given knowledge of the form of heteroscedasticity or autocorrelation)

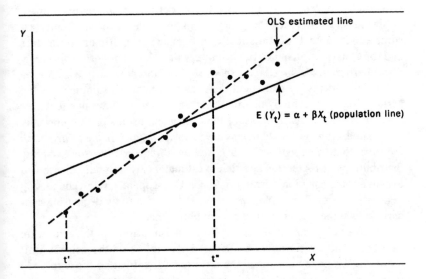

Figure 5.9. Illustration of the Implications of Autocorrelation: A Positive First-Order Autoregressive Process

are given the smallest weights in the sum to be minimized. For example, when heteroscedasticity is present, observations that are expected to have a large value for the error term because of a large variance for the error term at that level are given a small weight.[69] Finally, in the presence of heteroscedasticity or autocorrelation, the usual formula for estimating standard errors of coefficient estimators is incorrect and yields a biased estimator of the standard deviation of an OLS estimator.[70] Thus conventionally computed confidence intervals and conventional t tests for OLS estimators can no longer be justified (Berry & Feldman, 1985, pp. 77-78; Gujarati, 1988, pp. 325-326; Hanushek & Jackson, 1977, p. 146; Johnson et al., 1987, pp. 124-125).[71]

The Assumption That the Error Term Is Normally Distributed

We have already seen that several important properties of OLS coefficient estimators do not depend on the assumption that the error term is normally distributed. In particular, the Gauss-Markov theorem still holds, thereby ensuring that OLS coefficient estimators remain unbiased and efficient. The principal importance of the normality assumption is for tests of statistical significance for coefficient estimators and the construction of confidence intervals. *When estimation of regression coefficients is based on a small sample,* the normality assumption is required to justify statistical tests; as with a small sample, it is the assumption of a normally distributed error term that allows one to derive that the sampling distributions of the coefficient estimators are normally distributed. However, statisticians have shown, relying on the *central limit theorem,* that *when estimation is based on a large sample,* the sampling distributions of regression coefficient estimators are normally distributed even when the equation's error term is not. Consequently, when conducting regression, as one's sample size increases, one can show decreasing concern for whether the normality assumption is met.

The most common justification for the assumption that the error term in a regression is normally distributed also relies on the central limit theorem. We have interpreted the error term as reflecting the combined impact of a large number of independent variables that influence the dependent variable but are excluded from the regression, plus a random variable (see Equation 5.3). The central limit theorem (and extensions) demonstrate that with only rare exceptions, the distribution of the sum of a set of independent random variables approaches normality as the number of variables in the sum approaches infinity (Greene, 1990, p. 109; Gujarati, 1988, p. 90; Hanushek & Jackson, 1977, p. 335). Thus, to the extent that the error term approximates the sum of an infinite number of independent random variables, we can justify assuming that the error term is normally distributed. In practice, however, it is difficult to defend the claim that the excluded variables constituting a regression's error term are independent. Fortunately, there are tests for departures of the error term from normality. Fox (1984, pp. 174-175) recommends a visual inspection of graphs of regression residuals to detect large departures from normality. There are also formal statistical tests of the null hypothesis that the distribution of residuals is normal.[72]

6. CONCLUSION

Although most social scientists can recite the formal definitions of the various regression assumptions, many have little appreciation of the substantive meanings of these assumptions. And unless the meanings of these assumptions are understood, regression analysis almost inevitably will be a rigid exercise in which a handful of independent variables are cavalierly inserted into a standard linear additive regression and coefficients are estimated. Although such an exercise may occasionally produce results that are worth believing, it will do so only when an analyst is very lucky. The use of regression analysis to generate substantive conclusions that are *regularly* worth believing requires that users consider (a) whether each of the assumptions of regression is likely met in each specific research project at hand and, when some are not met, (b) the implications of these violations. This monograph was written to encourage students to avoid thinking of the regression assumptions as a list of phrases that must be memorized, and instead think of them as a vital set of conditions the applicability of which must be explicitly analyzed each time regression analysis is utilized.

NOTES

1. Of course, a wide range of assumptions must be made any time empirical research is used to test hypotheses, whether (a) that research is experimental or nonexperimental, and (b) it relies on quantitative methods (e.g., probit, logit, or two-stage least squares) or qualitative approaches (e.g., a comparative case study). The only issue is whether the analyst is aware of what these assumptions are.

2. For an introduction to regression analysis, see monographs by Lewis-Beck (1980) and Berry and Feldman (1985). More comprehensive treatments of regression are available in a wide variety of econometrics books; good intermediate texts have been written by Kelejian and Oates (1989), Gujarati (1988), Johnson, Johnson, and Buse (1987), Wonnacott and Wonnacott (1979) and Hanushek and Jackson (1977); at a more advanced level are texts by Greene (1990), Kmenta (1986), and Judge et al. (1985).

3. Throughout this monograph, when a variable has two subscripts, the first is used to identify a single variable within a *set* of variables each of which is represented by the same symbol (e.g., X). But when a variable is denoted by a distinct symbol, only one subscript is needed to identify a particular observation, or a specific value that the variable assumes. Thus, although I denote the independent variables in a k-regressor model by X_1, $X_2, \ldots, X_k$, I label the single independent variable in a bivariate model by X.

4. In contrast, the presence of the error term in the regression model, along with the assumptions about it to be reviewed below, mandates that the regression model is assumed to be deterministic only of the *means* of the conditional distributions of Y for fixed values of the independent variables.

5. To simplify the discussion, it is assumed that the explanatory variables in the true model have linear and additive effects on the dependent variable.

6. A *dichotomous* (or *dummy* or *binary*) variable is one with only two possible values. A *quantitative* (or *interval-level*) variable is one for which (a) the numbers assigned to

objects rank the objects according to how much they possess of some property, and (b) for any pair of objects, the difference between their scores accurately reflects the difference in the amount of the property they possess. Quantitative variables can be either continuous or discrete. *Continuous* variables are ones that can take on any numerical value. In contrast, *discrete* variables can assume only a finite number of specified values.

7. Note that for any two variables, V_1 and V_2, $COV(V_{1j}, V_{2j}) = 0$ if and only if $\rho_{12} = 0$ (where ρ_{12} denotes the correlation between V_1 and V_2). This is true because $\rho_{12} = COV(V_{1j}, V_{2j})/\sigma_1\sigma_2$, where σ_1 and σ_2 denote the standard deviations of V_1 and V_2, respectively.

If one could sample repeatedly independent variable values *fixed* by the analyst, assumption A5 would not be necessary, because in the case of fixed independent variables this assumption is guaranteed to be satisfied when assumption A4 (that the mean of the error term is zero) holds true. (For a development of the regression model for fixed regressors—and without assumption A5—see Wonnacott & Wonnacott, 1979, chap. 2.) But it is rare that social scientists are in position to fix the values of independent variables (as can be done in an experimental setting); they usually must accept whatever values the cases they observe happen to have; thus (to use the technical terminology) we develop the regression model allowing the independent variables to be *stochastic* or *random*.

8. When combined with the normality assumption (A8), A7 implies that ε_j and ε_h are *independent*.

9. The *maximum likelihood method* is one example of an alternative estimation strategy. Fortunately, if the Gauss-Markov assumptions hold, maximum likelihood estimators are identical to OLS estimators.

10. Isabelle Romieu and Walter Willett provided the data used to construct the population equation. No substantive conclusions about the factors determining weight should be drawn from my analysis, as Romieu and Willett's data (analyzed in Romieu et al., 1988) have been artificially "rigged" to illustrate the implications of regression assumptions.

11. As the full population consists of 134 women, strictly speaking, the dependent variable in the equation is discrete—in violation of assumption A1. But, having 134 distinct values, this discrete variable closely approximates continuousness.

12. No information about metabolic rate was included in the Romieu et al. (1988) data. Metabolic rate is typically defined as the energy output of an individual under standardized resting conditions (Garrow, 1974). But given that an indicator of metabolic rate had to be generated artificially, I was free to establish my own unit: the lucky.

13. This is because for any independent variable X in a regression equation, the slope of the relationship between X and the expected value of the dependent variable at any value of X, X^*, is the derivative of the equation with respect to X, at X^*.

14. For an extensive discussion of interaction effects in regression models, see Jaccard, Turrisi, and Wan (1990).

15. To be technically correct, these properties of OLS estimators hold only if assumption A5 is strengthened to require that for each X_i, X_i is distributed *independent* of ε; if X_i is merely *uncorrelated* with ε, the properties hold only for large samples (see, e.g., Gujarati, 1988, p. 57). (Two variables are termed *independent* if knowledge of the value of one variable for an observation would offer absolutely no assistance in predicting the value of the observation on the other variable. Two variables can be uncorrelated but *not* independent if there is some nonlinear relationship between the two.)

16. Unbiasedness is a so-called small-sample property of an estimator. Small-sample properties hold regardless of the sample size. In some cases, a biased estimator will be

consistent. A consistent estimator is one for which both bias and variance approach zero *as the sample size approaches infinity.*

17. Therefore, each of the probability distributions in Figure 4.1 can be termed a sampling distribution for θ. (For a clear discussion of the meaning of a sampling distribution, see Mohr, 1990, chap. 3.)

18. In other situations, we might have *panel data*—an observation for each of a set of cross-sectional units at multiple points in time—thereby undertaking what is called *pooled* regression analysis. Stimson (1985) offers an introduction to pooled regression; Hsiao (1986) provides a more advanced treatment.

19. For more detailed discussions of the effects of high multicollinearity, see Gujarati (1988, pp. 288-298), Johnson et al. (1987, pp. 265-268), Berry and Feldman (1985, pp. 40-42), and Hanushek and Jackson (1977, pp. 86-91).

20. Given the expression for ε_j in Equation 5.3, assumption A5 requires that $\delta_0 + (\Sigma_{i=1}^m \delta_i Z_{ij}) + R_j$ is uncorrelated with each independent variable. But δ_0, being a constant, and R_j, being a random variable, are uncorrelated with every variable. Therefore, assumption A5 requires that $\Sigma_{i=1}^m \delta_i Z_{ij}$ be uncorrelated with each independent variable.

21. When the dependent variable in a regression model affects one or more of the independent variables, a multiequation model—such as the system of equations formed by 5.4 and 5.5—is more appropriate. For estimation of such a model to be appropriate, the model must be *identified,* but even then OLS regression yields biased and inconsistent estimators of coefficients. Other techniques, such as two-stage least squares (2SLS), provide consistent estimators. For discussions of the requirements for identification and appropriate estimators for identified multiequation models, see Gujarati (1988, chaps. 17, 19), Berry (1984), and Hanushek and Jackson (1977, chap. 9).

22. The case of a specification error of *inclusion* (i.e., when a variable not in the frame of reference model is included in an estimation model) need not receive much attention here, as this type of specification error is easy to avoid. The following results should suffice. If a variable with no impact on a dependent variable in a population is included in an estimation regression, the expected value of the coefficient estimator for the variable is zero, and thus estimation based on a sample would likely leave the researcher unwilling to reject the null hypothesis that the coefficient is zero. (Of course, an unusual sample could result in a partial slope coefficient estimate for a mistakenly included variable that is significantly different from zero.) However, including an irrelevant variable in an estimation model results in inefficient OLS estimators for the *relevant* independent variables (Berry & Feldman, 1985, pp. 18-20; Deegan, 1976; Gujarati, 1988, pp. 404-405; Maddala, 1992, pp. 164-165).

23. These expected values for parameter estimators are obtained by running OLS regression on Equation 3.1 with data from the full population of 134 women but with METABOLISM excluded.

24. For other substantive examples in which an analyst is able to make reasonable inferences about the direction of bias resulting from a specification error of exclusion, see Griliches (1957), Kmenta (1986, p. 446), and Maddala (1992, pp. 163-164).

25. For discussions of the value of prior knowledge in overcoming a multicollinearity problem, see Kelejian and Oates (1989, pp. 209-210), Gujarati (1988, pp. 302-303), and Berry and Feldman (1985, pp. 47-48).

26. See Gujarati (1988, pp. 413-415) for further analysis of this multicollinearity problem—and other problems—with the nested model approach.

27. This is consistent with the earlier analysis of the implications of specification errors of exclusion that noted that when all excluded variables are uncorrelated with each included variable, partial slope coefficient estimators are unbiased.

28. The logic is similar in the multivariate case.

29. Greene (1990, p. 772) and Dubin and Rivers (1989-1990, pp. 364-366, 387-388) point out that this result is quite "general," but discuss some conditions under which it is guaranteed to hold. Dubin and Rivers actually derive the result.

30. For definitions of these terms, see Note 6.

31. For a provocative argument by a political scientist that many concepts studied by scholars in his discipline (e.g., voter preferences, political party identification) are fundamentally *non*continuous, and that, consequently, regression analysis is often inappropriate, see King (1989).

32. One could conceive of the measurement of length to the nearest fraction of an inch as involving *measurement error due to categorization*—a topic discussed later in this chapter.

33. Qualitative variables are also called *nominal* or *categorical*.

34. There are subtle differences in terminology in the literature. Many use the term *qualitative* to refer to unordered discrete variables with *two* or more categories, thereby making a dichotomous variable one kind of qualitative variable. Also, some use the term *qualitative* to refer to discrete variables with either unordered or ordered values.

35. A model in which all regressors are dichotomous is termed an *analysis of variance*.

36. Consequently, a regression model with a dependent variable that must be either 0 or 1 is called a linear *probability* model (Aldrich & Nelson, 1984, pp. 12-19).

37. Probit and logit are also appropriate with a discrete dependent variable having three or more values; logit is applicable when the values are unordered, whereas probit assumes ordered categories.

38. To be more precise, a typical random measurement error model would specify that $I_j = \delta + \mu T_j + v_j$, where the following assumptions hold: $\delta = 0$, $\mu = 1$, $E(v_j | T_j) = 0$, and $COV(T_j, v_j) = 0$ (see Carmines & Zeller, 1979, pp. 30-32; Gujarati, 1988, p. 416; Namboodiri, Carter, & Blalock, 1975, p. 539).

39. This is because when (a) $Y_j' = \delta + \mu Y_j + v_j$ (where the assumptions of Note 38 hold), (b) $COV(\varepsilon_j, v_j) = 0$, and (c) Y' is used to measure the dependent variable in Equation 2.2, the resulting equation can be rearranged to yield

$$\mu Y_j = (\alpha - \delta) + \beta_1 X_{1j} + \beta_2 X_{2j} + \ldots + \beta_k X_{kj} + (\varepsilon_j - v_j),$$

an equation (with an error term $\varepsilon_j - v_j$) that satisfies the Gauss-Markov assumptions if Equation 2.2 does. In effect, ε and v combine into a single disturbance term that behaves just like the error term ε in Equation 2.2.

40. In particular, $E(b) = \beta \cdot r_{XX}$, where r_{XX} is the reliability of the indicator for X (Berry & Feldman, 1985, p. 29).

41. Of course, when survey data produce indicators with NRME, there is also likely to be some *random* measurement error present. For instance, the assumption that *all* individuals underreport their true weight by *exactly* 10% is unlikely to be true. More plausible is the assumption that there is a *tendency* for respondents to underreport their weight by 10%, but that reported weight is also influenced by a random disturbance term, v, according to the equation

$$\text{WEIGHT}_j' = (.90)\text{WEIGHT}_j + v_j,$$

where $E(v_j|\text{WEIGHT}_j) = 0$ and $\text{COV}(\text{WEIGHT}_j, v_j) = 0$. Purposeful misrepresentation of weight would result in the nonrandom component of the measurement error, whereas carelessness in reading weight measurements on a scale and poor memory of scale readings might lead to the random component.

42. Namboodiri et al. (1975, pp. 579-581) refer to this as measurement error due to *classification*.

43. In a linear probability model (see Note 36), the partial slope coefficient for an independent variable, X_i, can be interpreted as the change in the probability that $Y = 1$ associated with a unit increase in X_i when all other independent variables are held constant.

44. The third example is Greene's (1990, p. 724).

45. When censoring of a dependent variable results in measurement error similar to the kind reflected in this illustration, the Tobit model is preferable to the regression model (see Amemiya, 1984; McDonald & Moffitt, 1980; Tobin, 1958). In one application of Tobit, a model's continuous dependent variable, Y (e.g., support for the cause), is assumed unobservable, and instead an indicator, M (e.g., amount contributed), of Y is employed, where M_j equals Y_j if Y_j is greater than some constant, c, but equals c if $Y_j \leq c$. The Tobit model can also be modified to deal with variables that are censored at the "high end" or at "both ends."

46. Most authors refer to such a model as intrinsically *linear*; adding the term *additive* makes the phrase more precise in meaning.

47. A model including a variable along with one or more powers of that variable is termed a *polynomial* model.

48. To confirm that this model takes the form of general Equation 5.16, we let $r = k = 1$, f and h be *identity* functions (i.e., ones that "map" a number onto itself), and $g_1(X_1) = 1/X_1$.

49. For discussions of these and other functional forms for nonlinear and/or nonadditive models that are linear and additive with respect to the parameters, see Johnson et al. (1987, pp. 239-255), Berry and Feldman (1985, pp. 57-71), and Hanushek and Jackson (1977, pp. 96-101).

50. For detailed discussions of the Cobb-Douglas function, see Gujarati (1988, pp. 189-192) and Kmenta (1986, pp. 511-512).

51. That is, a constant is added (or subtracted) from all scores on the independent variable so that the mean of the transformed variable is zero.

52. Given that the mean of X is zero, statisticians would recognize $E(X^3)/E(X^2)$ as m_3/m_2, where m_2 and m_3 are the second and third moments of X around its mean.

53. The formal measure of *skewness* of a distribution is equal to the third moment of the distribution about its mean divided by the cube of the distribution's standard deviation (Hoel, 1962, p. 77).

54. This is because a symmetric distribution has a skewness of zero, and the numerator of the formula defining skewness for a variable with a mean of zero is $E(X^3)$.

55. Recall that these slopes were calculated with Equation 3.2.

56. Equation 3.2 confirms that the slope of the relationship between fat intake and expected weight when FAT = 0 is $\beta_F + (2 \cdot \beta_{FF} \cdot 0) = \beta_F$.

57. Indeed, as a discussion of heteroscedasticity later in this chapter will show, one must also consider the possibility that the effects of independent variables vary depending

on the value of variables that influence the dependent variable but are *excluded* from the regression.

58. The following treatment is adapted from Theil (1971, p. 161).

59. For any set of k random variables $W_1, W_2, \ldots, W_k$, if $a_1, a_2, \ldots, a_k$ are constants, then $E(a_1 W_1 + a_2 W_2 + \ldots + a_k W_k) = a_1 E(W_1) + a_2 E(W_2) + \ldots + a_k E(W_k)$.

60. For any two variables X_1 and X_2 with zero mean, $COV(X_1, X_2) = E(X_1 \cdot X_2)$. That is, the covariance of two variables each with a mean of zero is the expected value of their product.

61. Some of the variables in Equation 3.1 would tend to be constant within any individual for weekly observations over a period of analysis of just a few years; for example, SMOKER might have to be excluded from the model for this reason. Other variables might have to be measured differently (e.g., average daily food intake might be measured for the previous week rather than the previous year).

62. This is a tenuous assumption. For example, health may be negatively related to fat intake. Also, if SMOKER did vary over the period of analysis, it too should be correlated with health.

63. This illustration is motivated by Wolf's (1989) study of gay priests.

64. The detection of autocorrelation is also based on the analysis of OLS regression residuals (Gujarati, 1988, pp. 368-379). The Durbin-Watson test is the most commonly used procedure. For discussions of this technique, and its limitations, see Gujarati (1988, pp. 375-379), Kennedy (1985, pp. 100-102, 105-106), Johnson et al. (1987, pp. 311-313), and Hanushek and Jackson (1977, pp. 164-168).

65. Another illustration of the role model respecification can play in overcoming heteroscedasticity is provided by Sigelman and Dometrius (1988). They contend that heteroscedasticity in a bivariate regression of (the Abney-Lauth measure of) gubernatorial influence on (Beyle's index of) formal power of the governor is a consequence of the exclusion of the variable "informal political resources" from the regression. This is because the impact of formal gubernatorial power on a governor's actual influence should get stronger as the amount of "informal" political resources at the governor's disposal increases.

66. In *higher*-order autoregressive processes, an error term's current value is determined at least partially by its predecessors two or more time periods ago (Hibbs, 1974; Ostrom, 1978, pp. 74-76).

67. For details about this form of autocorrelation, see Hibbs (1974) and Ostrom (1978). But see King (1989, pp. 185-187) for an argument that, in social science research, the assumption that autocorrelation takes a first-order autoregressive form is often inappropriate.

68. A large positive error term at time t'' after a series of primarily negative error terms would be due to an unusually large positive value for the random variable, u, at t''.

69. In the case of heteroscedasticity, GLS estimators can be determined through a procedure called *weighted least squares* (WLS), which is accomplished by transforming the original regression equation to one having a homoscedastic error term and then using OLS on the transformed equation (Berry & Feldman, 1985, pp. 87-88; Gujarati, 1988, pp. 322-325, 337-338; Wonnacott & Wonnacott, 1979, pp. 195-197).

70. However, it is possible to compute an alternative appropriate estimator of the standard error of an OLS estimator for a heteroscedastic model (Greene, 1990, pp. 403-405).

71. When autocorrelation takes the form, positive first-order autoregressive, the bias in the conventional estimators of the standard deviations of OLS estimators is negative, and therefore calculated confidence intervals tend to be narrower than they should be.

72. One such test relies on a Wald statistic; see Greene (1990, pp. 135, 329) for details.

REFERENCES

ALDRICH, J. H., and NELSON, F. D. (1984) Linear Probability, Logit, and Probit Models. Sage University Paper series on Quantitative Applications in the Social Sciences, 07-045. Beverly Hills, CA: Sage.

AMEMIYA, T. (1984) "Tobit models: A survey." Journal of Econometrics 24: 3-61.

BERRY, W. D. (1984) Nonrecursive Causal Models. Sage University Paper series on Quantitative Applications in the Social Sciences, 07-037. Beverly Hills, CA: Sage.

BERRY, W. D., and FELDMAN, S. (1985) Multiple Regression in Practice. Sage University Paper series on Quantitative Applications in the Social Sciences, 07-050. Beverly Hills, CA: Sage.

CARMINES, E. G., and ZELLER, R. A. (1979) Reliability and Validity Assessment. Sage University Paper series on Quantitative Applications in the Social Sciences, 07-017. Beverly Hills, CA: Sage.

CARTER, L. (1971) "Inadvertent sociological theory." Social Forces 50: 12-25.

DEEGAN, J., Jr. (1976) "The consequences of model misspecification in regression analysis." Multivariate Behavioral Research: 237-248.

DUBIN, J. A., and RIVERS, D. (1989-1990) "Selection bias in linear regression, logit, and probit models." Sociological Methods & Research 18: 360-390.

DYE, T. R. (1966) Politics, Economics, and the Public: Policy Outcomes in the American States. Chicago: Rand McNally.

FOX, J. (1984) Linear Statistical Models and Related Methods. New York: John Wiley.

GARROW, J. S. (1974) Energy Balance and Obesity in Man. New York: North-Holland.

GREENE, W. H. (1990) Econometric Analysis. New York: Macmillan.

GRILICHES, Z. (1957) "Specification bias in estimates of production functions." Journal of Farm Economics 39: 8-20.

GUJARATI, D. N. (1988) Basic Econometrics (2nd ed.). New York: McGraw-Hill.

HANUSHEK, E. A., and JACKSON, J. E. (1977) Statistical Methods for Social Scientists. New York: Academic Press.

HIBBS, D. A., Jr. (1974) "Problems of statistical estimation and causal inference in time-series regression models," in H. Costner (ed.) Sociological Methodology, 1973-1974. San Francisco: Jossey-Bass.

HOEL, P. G. (1962) Introduction to Mathematical Statistics (3rd ed.). New York: John Wiley.

HSIAO, C. (1986) Analysis of Panel Data. Cambridge: Cambridge University Press.

JACCARD, J., TURRISI, R., and WAN, C. K. (1990) Interaction Effects in Multiple Regression. Sage University Paper series on Quantitative Applications in the Social Sciences, 07-072. Newbury Park, CA: Sage.

JOHNSON, A. C., Jr., JOHNSON, M. B., and BUSE, R. C. (1987) Econometrics: Basic and Applied. New York: Macmillan.

JUDGE, G. G., et al. (1985) The Theory and Practice of Econometrics (2nd ed.). New York: John Wiley.

KELEJIAN, H. H., and OATES, W. E. (1989) Introduction to Econometrics (3rd ed.). New York: Harper & Row.

KENNEDY, P. (1985) A Guide to Econometrics (2nd ed.). Cambridge: MIT Press.

KING, G. (1989) Unifying Political Methodology: The Likelihood Theory of Statistical Inference. Cambridge: Cambridge University Press.

KMENTA, J. (1986) Elements of Econometrics (2nd ed.). New York: Macmillan.

LEWIS-BECK, M. S. (1980) Applied Regression: An Introduction. Sage University Paper series on Quantitative Applications in the Social Sciences, 07-022. Beverly Hills, CA: Sage.

LUSKIN, R. C. (1991) "Abusis non tollit usum: Standardized coefficients, correlations and R^2s." American Journal of Political Science 35: 1032-1046.

MADDALA, G. S. (1992) Introduction to Econometrics (2nd ed.). New York: Macmillan.

McDONALD, J. F., and MOFFITT, R. A. (1980) "The uses of tobit analysis." Review of Economics and Statistics 62: 318-321.

MOHR, L. B. (1990) Understanding Significance Testing. Sage University Paper series on Quantitative Applications in the Social Sciences, 07-073. Newbury Park, CA: Sage.

NAMBOODIRI, N. K., CARTER, L. F., and BLALOCK, H. M., Jr. (1975) Applied Multivariate Analysis and Experimental Designs. New York: McGraw-Hill.

ODLAND, J. (1988) Spatial Autocorrelation. Newbury Park, CA: Sage.

OSTROM, C. W., Jr. (1978) Time Series Analysis: Regression Techniques. Sage University Paper series on Quantitative Applications in the Social Sciences, 07-009. Beverly Hills, CA: Sage.

PRYOR, F. L. (1968) Public Expenditures in Communist and Capitalist Nations. Homewood, IL: Irwin.

RAO, P., and MILLER, R. L. (1971) Applied Econometrics. Belmont, CA: Wadsworth.

ROMIEU, I., et al. (1988) "Energy intake and other determinants of relative weight." American Journal of Clinical Nutrition 47: 406-412.

SCHROEDER, L. D., SJOQUIST, P. L., and STEPHAN, P. E. (1986) Understanding Regression Analysis: An Introductory Guide. Sage University Paper series on Quantitative Applications in the Social Sciences, 07-057. Beverly Hills, CA: Sage.

SIGELMAN, L., and DOMETRIUS, N. C. (1988) "Governors as chief administrators: The linkage between formal powers and informal influence." American Politics Quarterly 16: 157-170.

STIMSON, J. A. (1985) "Regression in space and time: A statistical essay." American Journal of Political Science 29: 914-947.

SUDMAN, S. (1976) Applied Sampling. New York: Academic Press.

THEIL, H. (1971) Principles of Econometrics. New York: John Wiley.

TOBIN, J. (1958) "Estimation of relationships for limited dependent variables." Econometrica 26: 24-36.

WOLF, J. (1989) Gay Priests. San Francisco: Harper & Row.

WONNACOTT, R. J., and WONNACOTT, T. H. (1979) Econometrics (2nd ed.). New York: John Wiley.

ABOUT THE AUTHOR

WILLIAM D. BERRY is Professor of Political Science at Florida State University. He earned his Ph.D. at the University of Minnesota, and has taught courses in statistics and research methodology at Florida State University and the University of Kentucky. His major areas of research are public policy and American state politics. He has published numerous articles in such scholarly journals as *American Political Science Review, American Journal of Political Science, Journal of Politics,* and *Social Science Quarterly.* He is coauthor of *Understanding United States Government Growth: An Empirical Analysis of the Post-War Era* (Praeger, 1987) and *Multiple Regression in Practice* (Sage, 1985), and author of *Nonrecursive Causal Models* (Sage, 1984).